home-cooked comforts

oven bakes, casseroles, & other one-pot dishes

home-cooked comforts

Laura Washburn

photography by Martin Brigdale

RYLAND
PETERS
& SMALL
LONDON NEW YORK

Design and Photographic Art Direction Steve Painter
Senior Commissioning Editor Julia Charles
Production Controller Toby Marshall
Art Director Leslie Harrington
Publishing Director Alison Starling

Food Stylist Linda Tubby
Prop Stylist Roisin Nield
Indexer Hilary Bird

First published in the United States in 2010 by Ryland Peters & Small Inc.
519 Broadway, 5th Floor
New York, NY 10012
www.rylandpeters.com

10 9 8 7 6 5 4 3 2 1

Library of Congress Cataloging-in-Publication Data

Washburn, Laura.
  Home-cooked comforts : oven-bakes, casseroles, and other one-pot dishes / Laura Washburn ; photography by Martin Brigdale.
       p. cm.
  Includes index.
  ISBN 978-1-84975-037-0
  1. Casserole cookery. 2. One-dish meals. 3. Cookery, International. I. Title.
  TX693.W43 2010
  641.8'21--dc22

2010012077

Notes
• All spoon measurements are level, unless otherwise specified.
• All eggs are large, unless otherwise specified. It is recommended that free-range eggs be used. Uncooked or partially cooked eggs should not be served to the very young, the very old, those with compromised immune systems, or to pregnant women.
• Ovens should be preheated to the specified temperature. Recipes in this book were tested using a regular oven. If using a fan-assisted oven, we strongly recommend that you follow the manufacturer's instructions for adjusting cooking times and/or temperatures.

contents

The comforts of home cooking

On any given, usually frantic, day the thought of something bubbling away in the kitchen can seem like shelter in a storm. The pace of life has become so frenetic for everyone, everywhere, it seems. I often retreat to my pots and pans, seeking solace in the stockpot. What better way to take some speed off the pace of life by spending just a little time in the kitchen, making something warming and comforting?

In this busy world, it is often hard to find time for the simple things, such as preparing a nice meal for family and friends. Even as someone with food preparation in my job description, as a working parent, I struggle to find the time more often than I care to admit. But the recipes presented in this book are intended to offer respite for the harried. They are designed to make it simple to slow down and savor something delicious, with dishes that can go straight from stovetop or oven to the table. Written with busy people in mind, many of the recipes can be quickly assembled, then left to simmer or bake, leaving time for other occupations and most can be made in advance so you can cook when you do have time, for enjoyment later on. Most are as suitable for midweek suppers as they are for weekend entertaining and, because times and tastes are changing, some of the recipes offer suggestions for vegetarian variations.

But spending time in the kitchen is not only good for our frame of mind, it can be good for our bodies. Homemade food can be so much more wholesome, especially when meals are prepared from scratch. So ease of preparation is not the only consideration; the recipes in this book also offer a way to put nutritious food on the table. Personally, I take great comfort in knowing what goes into the food on my plate and I don't like to leave the cooking to a factory assembly line. Preparing a square meal is so much simpler than you think, why do anything else? For the most part, each recipe in this book is a one-pot meal, often requiring little more than a crisp green salad and some crusty bread to complete composition. Easy, delicious, nutritious; it's hard to do better than that.

These recipes also offer plenty of variety for when you want to spice things up. I always turn to my cookbooks to get out of my routine so I have tried to make this a collection of dishes inspired by cuisines from around the world. Alongside traditional family fare, there are also recipes for curries, Asian dishes, tagines, and favorites from the American Southwest. Not restaurant food, but the kinds of dishes eaten at home, making them straightforward for any cook to prepare regardless of skill, using ingredients that can be found in most supermarkets. Life probably isn't going to slow down anytime soon and cooking is a good antidote, I think; and a way to sidestep the chaos. So go on, home cook some comfort today.

meat

black bean and chorizo chili

This is not mouth-searingly hot like some recipes. Quite the opposite, and the addition of chorizo adds another layer of flavor but not necessarily heat. Serve with boiled rice and/or warmed tortillas, and a simple salad of sliced avocados sprinkled with lime juice and olive oil. If you have any leftovers, this chili also makes a nice alternative filling for the Vegetable Enchiladas on page 114.

9 oz. chorizo, finely chopped

2–3 tablespoons vegetable oil

1 large onion, diced

4 bell peppers, mixed red, yellow, and orange, diced

2 celery ribs, with leaves, diced

2 teaspoons dried hot pepper flakes

½ teaspoon cayenne pepper (optional)

2½ teaspoons ground cumin

2 teaspoons dried oregano

2 garlic cloves, finely chopped

9 oz. ground beef

1 cup red wine

2 cups beef stock or water

1 bay leaf

14-oz. can chopped tomatoes

2 x 14-oz. cans black beans, drained

a handful of fresh cilantro leaves, chopped

fresh red chiles, sliced and seeded (optional)

sea salt

sour cream, to serve

rice or flour tortillas, to serve

Serves 4

Put the chorizo in a small saucepan and set over medium heat. Cook until browned then transfer the chorizo to a plate lined with paper towels and set aside.

Heat 2 tablespoons of the oil in a large saucepan. Add the onions and cook for 2–3 minutes, until soft. Add the bell peppers and celery, season with a little salt, and cook for a further 3–5 minutes, until soft. Stir in the pepper flakes, cayenne (if using), cumin, oregano, and garlic and cook, stirring, for 1 minute. Add the ground beef and cook for 5–7 minutes, stirring occasionally, until browned. Season with a little more salt.

Add the wine and cook for 1 minute, then stir in the stock, bay leaf, tomatoes, and beans. Cover, reduce the heat, and simmer for 15 minutes. Taste for seasoning and chile heat and adjust as necessary. Continue simmering, uncovered, for a further 20–30 minutes.

When ready to serve, stir in the cilantro. Scatter over the fresh chiles (if using) and serve the sour cream on the side. Rice and/or warmed flour tortillas make a good accompaniment.

Hungarian goulash

This recipe was given to me by a Hungarian friend, who is an exceptional cook. It took a few tries to get mine to taste as good as hers. Apparently, she makes it just like her grandmother does, but it was very difficult to extract the method for their "secret" touch. It has something to do with feeling; theirs is surely superlative. She did explain that Hungarians always cook with generous doses of spice and perhaps add more salt than is recommended so feel free to do the same. This is traditionally served with wide ribbon egg noodles but works well with pasta such as tagliatelle.

1 tablespoon vegetable oil

2 onions, diced

1 red bell pepper, seeded and diced

1 green bell pepper, seeded and diced

1 teaspoon caraway seeds

2 generous teaspoons paprika, sweet or hot, or half and half

1½ lbs. stewing beef, cut into small cubes

3 large ripe tomatoes, peeled, cored, seeded, and chopped

1 tablespoon tomato paste

3 carrots, diced

1½ cups beef stock

2 bay leaves

14-oz. can kidney beans, drained

a large handful of fresh parsley leaves, chopped

sea salt and freshly ground black pepper

wide egg noodles, to serve

Serves 4

Heat the oil in a large saucepan. Add the onions and bell peppers and cook until soft. Season with a little salt and add the caraway seeds and paprika. Cook for 1 minute. Add the cubed beef. Cook, stirring occasionally, for 2–3 minutes, until browned. Season with a little more salt if liked.

Add the tomatoes, tomato paste, carrots, stock, and bay leaves, and season lightly. Simmer, uncovered, for at least 40 minutes. Add the kidney beans and cook for 10 minutes more (do not be tempted to add the beans any earlier as they will become tough if overcooked.)

Sprinkle with the parsley and serve spooned over noodles.

steak, leek, and mushroom pie with Guinness

Pies are a wonderful thing. They look and taste fantastic, and are really straightforward to make, especially if you leave out the bottom layer of pastry, which I always do. Serve with plenty of creamy mashed potatoes and peas, if liked.

1 tablespoon vegetable oil

1½ lbs. stewing beef, cut into bite-size pieces

2 trimmed leeks, sliced into ½-inch rounds

1 onion, coarsely chopped

2 large carrots, peeled and diced

9 oz. mushrooms, coarsely chopped

4 oz. thick-sliced bacon, coarsely chopped

1 teaspoon dried thyme

2 garlic cloves, crushed

2 tablespoons all-purpose flour

12-oz. can Guinness

2 tablespoons Worcestershire sauce

1 bay leaf

a large handful of fresh parsley leaves, chopped

13-oz. package puff pastry, defrosted if frozen

melted butter or milk, to brush

sea salt and freshly ground black pepper

a flameproof casserole dish
a 12 x 8 inch baking dish

Serves 4–6

Preheat the oven to 325°F.

Heat the oil in a large flameproof casserole dish. Add the beef and cook, stirring, for 2–3 minutes, until just browned. Remove the meat from the casserole dish, season and set aside.

Add the leeks, onion, and carrots to the pan, adding a little more oil if necessary. Cook over low heat for about 3 minutes, until softened. Add the mushrooms, bacon, and thyme and cook for a further 2–3 minutes. Season well. Add the garlic and cook for 1 minute.

Return the beef to the casserole dish, add the flour, stir to coat the meat in the flour and cook for 2–3 minutes. Pour in the Guinness and Worcestershire sauce. Add the bay leaf and parsley and pour in sufficient cold water to just cover. Stir to mix, cover with a lid, and bake in the preheated oven for about 1½ hours.

Remove the casserole dish from the oven and increase the oven temperature to 400°F.

Transfer the beef mixture to the baking dish. Roll out the pastry and use to cover the pie filling. It should look rustic, so fold over the edges and crimp roughly with your fingers. Using a sharp knife, and starting at the top edge, make lengthwise slits on the diagonal, in stripes about ¼ inch apart, all the way across. Brush with melted butter or milk and bake in the preheated oven for about 25–30 minutes, until golden. Serve immediately with mashed potatoes and peas on the side.

beef and zucchini gratin

It's not possible to have too many recipes for ground beef, and this is a great one. The goat cheese lifts this out of the ordinary but, as the tangy flavor is not to everyone's taste, sharp cheddar is a nice option if you prefer. This is ideal for feeding a crowd and makes a pleasant change from lasagne. Serve with a mixed salad and crusty bread.

In a large skillet, combine the onions and 1 tablespoon of the oil. Cook over medium heat for about 3–5 minutes, until soft. Stir in the thyme, oregano, pepper flakes, and garlic and cook, stirring, for about 1 minute. Add the wine, cook for 1 further minute, then add the beef. Cook for 5–8 minutes, stirring occasionally, until the beef is browned. Stir in the tomatoes and sugar and season well. Reduce the heat, cover, and simmer gently for at least 15 minutes.

Preheat the oven to 400°F.

Meanwhile, prepare the zucchini. Line a baking sheet with paper towels. Working in batches, heat some of the oil in a large nonstick skillet. When hot, add the zucchini rounds and sauté, in a single layer. When just golden, turn and brown the other side. Transfer to the lined baking sheet. Continue until all the zucchini are browned.

Stir 2 tablespoons of the sour cream into the beef mixture. Put the remaining sour cream in a bowl, crumble in the goat cheese, and season with salt and pepper. Mix well. Set aside.

To assemble, arrange one-third of the zucchini in an even layer on the bottom of the baking dish. Sprinkle with salt and one-third of the grated cheese. Top with half of the beef mixture, spread evenly. Repeat the zucchini and beef layer. Finish with a final zucchini layer. Season with salt, then spread with an even layer of the sour cream topping. Sprinkle over the remaining cheese. Bake in the preheated oven for about 30 minutes, until the top is golden brown.

1 onion, finely chopped

about ½ cup olive oil

1 teaspoon dried thyme

1 teaspoon dried oregano

¼ teaspoon dried hot pepper flakes

2 garlic cloves, crushed

½ cup dry white or red wine

1 lb. ground beef

14-oz. can chopped tomatoes

a pinch of sugar

4 lbs. zucchini (about 6), sliced into ½-inch rounds

1 scant cup sour cream

2 oz. soft goat cheese, crumbled

1 cup grated Gruyère or cheddar

1–2 tablespoons milk

sea salt and freshly ground black pepper

a 10 x 8 inch deep-sided baking dish

Serves 4–6

Asian beef braise with bok-choy

A different kind of beef stew, this recipe has flavors of the Orient but is easy to make at home with ordinary Western utensils. If you can find cubes of frozen chopped ginger at your supermarket, they will come in handy here, or in any recipe, which is why I like to keep them around. Serve this with any kind of Asian noodle—egg noodles will do the trick, or try something unusual like Japanese soba noodles or thick Ho Fun noodles.

2 tablespoons vegetable oil

1¼ lbs. braising steak, cut into bite-size pieces

1 garlic clove, crushed

1 large shallot, sliced

1-inch piece of fresh ginger, peeled and grated

3 cups beef stock

½ cup Chinese rice wine

½ cup hoisin sauce

¼ teaspoon ground cumin

1 star anise

1 fresh red chile, sliced

freshly squeezed juice of 1 tangerine (or ½ an orange)

1 teaspoon honey

4–6 bok-choy

Asian noodles, to serve

Serves 4

Heat the oil in a large saucepan. Add the steak and cook until browned. Transfer to a plate, season with salt and set aside.

Add the garlic, shallot, and ginger to the saucepan and cook, stirring constantly for 1 minute. Add the stock, rice wine, hoisin sauce, cumin, star anise, chile, tangerine juice, and honey. Stir to blend and bring to a boil. Return the steak to the saucepan, reduce the heat, and simmer very gently, uncovered, for 1–1½ hours, until the meat is tender. Taste and adjust the seasoning.

Core the bok-choy. Cut the white part into ½-inch slices; leave the greens large or cut in half. Add the white part to the saucepan, increase the heat, and cook until just tender, 3–4 minutes. Add the greens and cook until just wilted, about 2–3 minutes more. Serve immediately with Asian noodles of your choice.

Thai red beef curry

This is a truly straightforward curry recipe. There are many brands of curry paste available, some better than others, but if you find a good one, this will taste remarkably authentic. In reality, you could simply stop at the curry paste and coconut milk, but I like to jazz up the ready-made sauce with even more lemongrass and ginger. And, the fish sauce and palm sugar give the finished dish more depth. Use this as a blueprint recipe for any Thai red curry and experiment with different ingredients in place of the beef. Boneless chicken or shrimp work well, as do a mixture of vegetables such as baby corn, eggplant, sweet potato, and broccoli. Serve with basmati rice, either steamed or boiled.

1 tablespoon vegetable oil

1½ lbs. sirloin steak, sliced into thin strips

4 tablespoons Thai red curry paste

2 x 14-oz. cans coconut milk

½ lemongrass stalk, white part only, very finely chopped

1–2 tablespoons Thai fish sauce, to taste

1-inch piece of fresh ginger, peeled and grated

1 tablespoon palm sugar or runny honey

10 oz. green beans, cut into 1-inch lengths

steamed basmati rice, to serve

Serves 4

Heat the oil in a large saucepan. Add the beef and cook for 2–3 minutes, stirring, until just browned. Add the curry paste and continue cooking for 1–2 minutes, stirring occasionally to coat the meat.

Add the coconut milk, lemongrass, 1 tablespoon of the fish sauce, ginger, and sugar. Stir well, reduce the heat, and simmer gently for 15 minutes. Taste and add the remaining tablespoon of fish sauce if necessary. Continue simmering, uncovered, for about 15 minutes more.

Add the green beans, part cover, and simmer gently for about 10 minutes more until the beans are just tender. Serve immediately with plenty of rice.

tamale pie

1 tablespoon vegetable oil

1 onion, finely chopped

1 green bell pepper, chopped

1 lb. ground pork or beef

2 teaspoons chili powder

1 teaspoon ground cumin

½ teaspoon cayenne pepper
(optional)

½ teaspoon allspice

14-oz. can kidney beans or
black beans, drained

14-oz. can chopped tomatoes

½ cup pitted black olives, sliced

1 cup corn kernels, canned
or frozen

1 tablespoon Worcestershire
sauce

Tabasco sauce (optional)

sea salt and freshly ground
black pepper

For the topping

1 cup all-purpose flour

1 cup cornmeal

2 teaspoons baking powder

¼ teaspoon salt

a pinch of sugar

3 tablespoons melted butter

¾ cup milk or buttermilk

1 egg, beaten

1 small fresh green chile,
very finely chopped

½ cup grated mild cheddar

a 12 x 8 inch baking dish

Serves 4–6

This is topped with a golden cornbread topping, instead of the traditional masa harina, which is not always easy to obtain. It's a cinch to prepare and is a great recipe to fiddle. You can use leftover roast meat instead of ground pork; either beef or pork, or both. If you have an abundant supply of fresh chiles, try some instead of the green bell pepper, or simply add as well. A handful of chopped jalapeños from a jar are good if you want to add a real kick. Serve with sour cream and a salad of thinly sliced tomatoes and red onions, dressed with oil, lime juice, and chopped fresh cilantro.

Preheat the oven to 375°F.

Heat the oil in a large skillet. Add the onion and green bell pepper and cook for about 5 minutes, until soft. Season and add the ground pork, chili powder, cumin, cayenne, and allspice. Cook, stirring often, until browned.

Stir in the beans, tomatoes, olives, corn, and Worcestershire sauce. Reduce the heat and simmer, uncovered, for about 10–15 minutes.

Meanwhile, prepare the topping. Put the flour, cornmeal, baking powder, salt, and sugar in a bowl and stir to combine. Stir in the melted butter, milk, and egg and stir just until blended. Stir in the chile and cheese. Add an extra spoonful of milk if the mixture seems dry.

Taste the pork mixture and adjust the seasoning if necessary. Add some Tabasco if it is not hot enough. Spoon into the baking dish and spread evenly. Drop the cornmeal mixture in spoonfuls on top, spreading evenly to cover.

Bake in the preheated oven for about 30 minutes, until the topping is golden brown. Serve immediately.

Variation: For a vegetarian version, replace the ground pork with an additional can of beans and add 1–2 diced zucchini, cooked along with the onion and bell pepper.

braised pot roast with red wine, rosemary, and bay leaves

This is the sort of food that makes you long for cold wintry days, when it is nice to stay indoors and simmer something slowly—heating the kitchen and filling the house with rich, warming aromas. It also has appeal for the lazy spendthrift as preparation is minimal and the cut of meat is inexpensive. There are several nice accompaniments for this: you could serve creamy mashed potatoes, soft polenta, or even macaroni baked in cream with plenty of Parmesan.

3 lbs. braising joint, such as beef brisket, tied

2 tablespoons olive oil

1 onion, halved and thinly sliced

2 celery ribs, thinly sliced

1 large carrot, thinly sliced and cut into half-moons

4 garlic cloves, peeled and sliced

6 oz. pancetta, finely chopped

750-ml bottle robust red wine, preferably Italian

14-oz. can chopped tomatoes

1 bay leaf, 2 large sprigs fresh rosemary, several sprigs fresh parsley, all firmly tied together in a bundle

3–4 tablespoons capers in brine, drained (optional)

sea salt and freshly ground black pepper

a flameproof casserole dish

Serves 6

Preheat the oven to 350°F.

Heat the oil in a large flameproof casserole dish. Add the beef and cook for about 8–10 minutes, until browned on all sides. Transfer the beef to a plate, season all over with salt and set aside.

Add the onion, celery, and carrot to the casserole dish and cook, stirring often, until browned. Add the garlic and pancetta and cook for 1 minute. Season, then add the wine and tomatoes and bring to a boil. Boil for 1 minute, then add the herb bundle. Return the browned beef to the casserole dish.

Cover and transfer to the preheated oven. After 1½ hours, remove the casserole dish from the oven and turn the beef over. Pour in some water if the liquid has reduced too much and add the capers, if using. Return to the oven and cook for a further 1½ hours, until the meat is tender.

Serve in slices with the sauce and vegetables spooned over the top and with the accompaniment of your choice.

meatloaf

A free-form meatloaf has a few advantages. There is more browned surface on the top, which is the part I like the most, and it looks nicer. This American classic simply must be served with mashed potatoes and gravy, and leftovers make the perfect sandwich filling.

1 onion, coarsely chopped

2 garlic cloves

1 celery rib, coarsely chopped

leaves from a small bunch of fresh parsley

2 tablespoons olive oil

1 lbs. ground beef

12 oz. ground pork

2 eggs, beaten

2 tablespoons milk

1 cup fresh bread crumbs (see note)

1 teaspoon dried thyme

2 teaspoons salt

½ teaspoon ground white pepper

1 teaspoon paprika

¼ cup chili sauce or ketchup

2–3 bay leaves, plus extra to garnish

5–6 bacon slices

sea salt and freshly ground black pepper

a heavy baking sheet or shallow roasting pan

Serves 6–8

Preheat the oven to 350°F.

Combine the onion, garlic, celery, and parsley in a food processor and pulse until minced.

Transfer the mixture to a skillet, add the oil and cook over low heat for 5–7 minutes, until soft. Transfer to a large bowl and add the beef, pork, eggs, milk, bread crumbs, thyme, salt, pepper, paprika, and chili sauce. Mix well with your hands until well blended.

Form the mixture into an oval loaf shape, as if you were making bread. Put the bay leaves in the middle of the baking sheet and place the meatloaf on top. Arrange the bacon slices on top, at equal intervals.

Bake in the preheated oven for about 1½ hours, until browned and cooked through. Do check the meatloaf regularly and baste with the pan juices to keep it moist. Serve with mashed potatoes and gravy.

Note: The best way to obtain fresh bread crumbs is to use the end pieces from a sliced loaf, wholemeal or white but nothing with seeds. Simply tear into smaller pieces and put in the bowl of a food processor and processor to obtain crumbs. (The food processor is required for the onions in this recipe as well but do the bread crumbs first because they are a dry ingredient.)

oven-braised lamb shanks with potatoes and tomatoes

Anything that contains an entire bottle of wine cannot possibly be bad, and this is surely proof. It is based on a recipe for leg of lamb that cooks for seven hours. In the interest of using less energy, I have changed the cut of meat and reduced the cooking time, with great success. This is incredibly simple and utterly satisfying. And although it is rustic, it is impressive, so perfect for entertaining. To keep with the energy saving theme, serve by candlelight.

2 tablespoons olive oil

4 lamb shanks

3 onions, quartered

5 carrots, coarsely chopped

6 garlic cloves, sliced

4 anchovy fillets, finely chopped (optional)

750-ml bottle dry white wine

1 bay leaf, 1 large sprig of fresh thyme, 1 large sprig of fresh rosemary, several sprigs of fresh parsley, all firmly tied together in a bundle

2¼ lbs. new potatoes, quartered

6 fresh plum tomatoes, cored and coarsely chopped

sea salt and freshly ground black pepper

a flameproof casserole dish

Serves 4

Preheat the oven to 300°F.

Heat the oil in a large flameproof casserole dish. Add the lamb shanks and cook for about 7–10 minutes, until browned all over, turning halfway through. Transfer the lamb shanks to a dish, season generously with salt and set aside.

Add the onions and carrots to the casserole dish and cook for 3–5 minutes, until just browned. Add the garlic and anchovies, if using, and cook for 1 minute. Season well and add the wine. Bring to a boil and cook for 1 minute. Return the lamb shanks to the casserole dish and add the herb bundle, burying it in the liquid. Add water if necessary; the lamb should be almost completely submerged in liquid. Cover and cook in the preheated oven for 2 hours, checking occasionally, to ensure it does not reduce too much.

After 2 hours, top up with water if the liquid has greatly reduced, then add the potatoes and tomatoes and a good pinch of salt. Cook for 1 hour. Remove from the oven, taste, and adjust the seasoning if necessary. Remove the herb bundle before serving.

moussaka

Some recipes for this traditional Greek dish call for potatoes alongside the eggplants, and some have potatoes only. This one is all eggplant. Another departure here is the yogurt topping in place of the classic béchamel sauce. The result is a lighter finished dish, less toil for the cook and an even better flavor, if I do say so myself! This improves over time so is best made a day in advance, refrigerated, and baked when ready to serve.

1 onion, chopped

4–5 tablespoons olive oil

1 lb. ground lamb

2 garlic cloves, finely chopped

½ teaspoon ground allspice

¼ teaspoon ground cinnamon

2 teaspoons dried oregano

½ cup red wine

2 x 14-oz. cans chopped tomatoes

1 bay leaf, plus extra to garnish

a pinch of sugar

3 medium eggplants, sliced into ½-inch rounds

sea salt and freshly ground black pepper

For the topping

1½ cups Greek-style yogurt

2 eggs, beaten

6 oz. feta, crumbled

a large handful of fresh mint leaves, chopped

3 tablespoons grated Parmesan

a 12 x 8 inch baking dish

Serves 6

Combine the onion and 1 tablespoon of the oil in a large skillet. Cook the onion for about 3–5 minutes, until soft. Add the lamb, season well and cook, stirring, for about 5 minutes, until browned. Add the garlic, allspice, cinnamon, and oregano and cook for 1 minute. Add the wine and cook for 1 minute more. Add the tomatoes, bay leaf, and sugar and mix well. Let simmer gently, uncovered, while you prepare the eggplants.

Preheat the oven to 400°F.

Heat a few tablespoons of the oil in a large nonstick skillet. Add the eggplant slices in a single layer and sauté to brown slightly. Using tongs, turn and cook the other sides, then transfer to paper towels to drain. Work in batches, adding more oil as necessary, until all the eggplant slices are browned.

In a bowl, combine the yogurt, eggs, and feta and mix well with a fork until blended. Season well with salt and pepper and stir in the mint. Set aside.

To assemble the moussaka, arrange half of the lamb mixture on the bottom of the baking dish. Top with half of the eggplant slices. Repeat once more. Spread the yogurt mixture on top and level the surface. Sprinkle with the Parmesan and decorate with bay leaves.

Bake in the preheated oven for about 40–50 minutes, until golden brown and bubbling. Serve immediately.

spiced lamb tagine with prunes

Tagines may sound exotic, but they couldn't be easier to prepare. This recipe is a perfect example. It is simple and satisfying, perfect as a weeknight supper but equally suited for entertaining. Serve with couscous and a watercress salad dressed with extra virgin olive oil and freshly squeezed orange juice.

2 onions

2 tablespoons olive oil

1 teaspoon ground turmeric

1 teaspoon ground ginger

½ teaspoon freshly ground black pepper

a pinch of saffron threads

1 teaspoon ground cumin

½ teaspoon ground cinnamon

2¼ lbs. stewing lamb, cut into bite-size pieces

a small bunch of cilantro, firmly tied into a bundle with string

1 cup pitted soft prunes

2 tablespoons runny honey

sea salt and freshly ground black pepper

couscous, to serve

Serves 4

Finely chop 1 of the onions either by grating it on the coarse side of a grater or processing in a food processor. Put it in a large saucepan or flameproof casserole dish.

Add the oil, spices, and lamb. Cook over low heat for 2–3 minutes, stirring to coat the lamb in oil, until the mixture becomes aromatic. Season well with salt. Pour in sufficient water just to cover and add the cilantro bundle. Reduce the heat, cover, and simmer gently for 1½ hours.

Halve the remaining onion and slice into thin half moon slices. When the lamb is tender, remove with a slotted spoon and transfer to a dish. Cover and keep warm.

Add the sliced onion, prunes, and honey to the liquid in the saucepan. Cover and cook for about 15 minutes, until the onion is tender. Remove the lid and simmer for about 5–8 minutes to reduce the sauce slightly. Return the lamb to the pan and toss well. Serve spooned over couscous.

Mediterranean stuffed onions with rice

Onions make a nifty, and tasty, container for the gently spiced lamb filling. This dish is a fantastic all-season meal; in winter, serve it hot for something comforting and satisfying. When it's warmer, this can be served at room temperature, accompanied by a mixed leaf salad. Do be sure to season the stuffing mixture well or the finished dish will be bland.

8 large red or white onions

2–3 tablespoons olive oil

1 lb. ground lamb

2 garlic cloves, crushed

1 heaping tablespoon tomato paste

½ teaspoon ground cinnamon

2 tablespoons finely chopped fresh dill

2 tablespoons finely chopped fresh mint

½ cup dry white wine

1½ cups brown rice

1 egg, beaten

1 cup fresh bread crumbs (see note on page 26)

sea salt and freshly ground black pepper

a baking dish, large enough to take all the onions in a single layer

Serves 4

Slice the tops and bottoms off of the onions, taking only a little at the root end and more at the top. Use a melon baller to scoop out the insides, leaving 2–3 layers of the outer onion as a shell. Put the scooped-out onion flesh in a food processor and process until finely chopped.

Put 1 tablespoon of the oil in a large skillet and add 4 tablespoons of the chopped onions (the remainder can be frozen for use in other recipes.) Cook for 3–5 minutes, until soft. Add the lamb, season well, and cook for 5–7 minutes, stirring to break up the meat. Stir in the garlic, tomato paste, cinnamon, dill, mint, and wine and cook for 2–3 minutes, stirring. Taste and adjust the seasoning. Remove from the heat and let cool.

Preheat the oven to 400°F.

Add the rice in an even layer in the bottom of the baking dish. Brush the inside of the onion shells with oil and sprinkle with salt.

When the stuffing is cool enough to handle, stir in the bread crumbs and egg and about 2–3 tablespoons water. The mixture should be soft, but not soupy. Spoon the mixture into the onion shells, filling all the way to the top, mounding only slightly. Arrange the filled onions on top of the rice and brush the outsides with oil. Pour 2 cups water into the dish.

Bake in the preheated oven for 1–1½ hours, until the rice is cooked and the onions are browned. Keep an eye on the rice and begin testing it after 1 hour in the oven. You may need to add more water. Serve immediately or let cool to room temperature and serve with a mixed green salad on the side.

meatball tagine

This is an unusual but traditional Moroccan recipe. When prepared in a tagine (cooking vessel), the eggs are cooked in the dish with the meatballs, on top of the sauce. This recipe cooks the eggs separately, allowing for preparation in an ordinary straight-sided skillet. If you feel the need to add something green, add some frozen peas with the meatballs. This addition is not traditional, but tasty. Serve with bread to mop up the aromatic tomato sauce.

½ onion, coarsely chopped

a few sprigs of fresh parsley

a few sprigs of fresh cilantro

1 lb. ground lamb

1½ teaspoons sea salt

½ teaspoon ground white pepper

1 teaspoon ground cumin

1 teaspoon paprika

1 tablespoon fresh bread crumbs (see note on page 26)

4 eggs, to serve (optional)

For the sauce

1½ onions

a small handful of fresh parsley

2 garlic cloves

14-oz. can chopped tomatoes

1¼ cups stock (chicken, lamb, or vegetable) or water

1½ teaspoons ground cumin

1 teaspoon ground white pepper

¼ teaspoon ground cinnamon

¼–½ teaspoon cayenne pepper, to taste

a pinch of sugar

Serves 4

To make the meatballs, put the onion in a food processor with the parsley and cilantro. Process until finely chopped. Add the lamb and process, using the pulse button, to obtain a smooth paste. Transfer to a bowl.

Add the salt, pepper, cumin, paprika, and bread crumbs. Mix well with your hands to combine. Carefully form into walnut-size balls and transfer to a baking sheet. Cover and set aside.

To make the sauce, put the onions, parsley, and garlic in a food processor and process until finely chopped. Transfer to a shallow skillet large enough to hold the meatballs in a single layer. Add the tomatoes, stock, cumin, pepper, cinnamon, cayenne, and sugar. Stir and bring to a boil, then lower the heat and simmer, covered, for 15 minutes.

Nestle the meatballs in the sauce in a single layer. Cover and simmer for 20–30 minutes, until cooked through.

To serve, divide the meatballs and sauce between shallow soup plates or large bowls, arranging the meatballs in a ring around the perimeter. Poach or lightly fry the eggs if using (keep the yolks runny) and place one cooked egg in the middle of each bowl. Serve immediately.

sausage, pasta, and bean stew with greens

Easy to make and even easier to enjoy, this is truly a one-pot meal. It can be served as soon as the sausage and pasta are cooked, which doesn't take long at all, but the taste improves if made in advance. If using spicy sausage, you may not need to add the hot pepper flakes. To serve, simply put the pot on the table with a basket of crusty bread and offer extra finely grated Parmesan for sprinkling.

1 tablespoon olive oil

1 large onion, coarsely chopped

12 Italian- or Toulouse-style sausages (about 1¾ lbs.) cut into bite-size pieces

4 garlic cloves, sliced

¼–1 teaspoon dried hot pepper flakes, to taste

14-oz. can chopped tomatoes

1 cup red wine

1 bay leaf

4 oz. small pasta shapes, such as macaroni

about 6 oz. greens, such as curly kale, chard, or cavolo nero, shredded

14-oz. can cannellini beans, drained

a large handful of fresh basil leaves, chopped

sea salt and freshly ground black pepper

finely grated Parmesan, to serve

crusty bread, to serve

Serves 4–6

Heat the oil in a large saucepan. Add the onion and cook 3–5 minutes, until soft. Add the sausage and cook for about 5 minutes, until browned. Stir in the garlic and pepper flakes and cook for 1 minute.

Add the tomatoes, wine, and bay leaf and enough water to cover. Don't worry if it's soupy at this stage. Bring to a boil, then add the pasta and cook, uncovered, for about 10 minutes, until the pasta is al dente.

Meanwhile bring a separate large saucepan of lightly salted water to a boil. Add the greens and cook briefly just to blanch. Drain and set aside.

Add the blanched greens and beans to the sausage mixture and stir well. Simmer, uncovered, for a further 5 minutes. Taste and adjust the seasoning. Stir in the basil and serve sprinkled with finely grated Parmesan and plenty of crusty bread on the side.

pork stew with sweet potatoes, beans, and chile

The combination of sweet potato and chile here is fantastic, and it goes well with the melting texture of the pork. Like any stew, this improves with age but is flavorsome enough to serve the same day it was made. Crusty bread makes a good accompaniment.

Preheat the oven to 300°F.

Heat 1 tablespoon of the oil in a large flameproof casserole dish or saucepan. Add the onion and cook for 3–5 minutes, until soft. Stir in 1 teaspoon of the cumin and the oregano and cook for 2–3 minutes, until fragrant. Remove from the casserole dish and set aside.

Add the pork and the remaining tablespoon of oil and cook for 5–7 minutes, until browned all over. Stir in the honey, the remaining cumin, the cinnamon, garlic, and chile. Season with salt and mix well. Return the onions to the pan and add the tomatoes, stock, sweet potatoes, and bay leaf. Bring to a boil, then cover and transfer to the preheated oven. Cook for 40 minutes.

Remove from the oven and stir in the beans. Cover and return to the oven to cook for a further 20 minutes. Sprinkle with cilantro and serve with yogurt on the side, if liked, and crusty bread.

Variation: For a vegetarian version, omit the pork and add 1 diced butternut squash with the sweet potatoes and a 14-oz. can butter beans with the kidney beans. Reduce the cooking time from 40 minutes to 15 minutes.

2 tablespoons olive oil

1 large onion, chopped

2 teaspoons ground cumin

1½ teaspoons dried oregano

1½ lbs. pork shoulder, cubed

1 teaspoon runny honey

1 teaspoon ground cinnamon

2 garlic cloves, finely chopped

1 fresh red chile, seeded and thinly sliced

14-oz. can chopped tomatoes

2 cups chicken or vegetable stock

2–3 sweet potatoes (about 1¾ lbs.), peeled and cubed

1 bay leaf

14-oz. can kidney beans, drained

a large handful of fresh cilantro leaves, chopped

sea salt and freshly ground black pepper

Greek-style yogurt, to serve (optional)

Serves 4

ham and pasta bake with artichokes, olives, and sun-dried tomatoes

This pasta bake is so easy it hardly feels like cooking! It can also be used as a pantry clearing exercise if lots of jars and bottles are stacking up and not getting used. The recipe uses the most common items, but do feel free to experiment with any antipasto-style ingredient that happens to be lurking on your shelves and do not worry if quantities are not exact. Some jars are bigger than others and there is no need to be too precise here.

1 lb. dried pasta shells

5 oz. ham or salami, coarsely chopped

10-oz. jar marinated artichokes, drained and coarsely chopped

5 oz. sun-dried tomatoes, drained and coarsely chopped

½ cup pitted black olives

2 tablespoons drained capers

4–5 anchovy fillets, coarsely chopped (optional)

2 cups prepared marinara sauce

¾ cup heavy cream

1 teaspoon dried hot pepper flakes (optional)

⅔ cup grated mild cheddar or firm mozzarella

3 tablespoons grated Parmesan

sea salt and freshly ground black pepper

a 12 x 10 inch baking dish, oiled

Serves 4–6

Preheat the oven to 400°F.

Cook the pasta according to the package instructions. Drain well and tip into a large mixing bowl.

Add the ham, artichokes, sun-dried tomatoes, olives, capers, and anchovies, if using, to the pasta and mix well.

In a separate bowl, stir together the marinara sauce and cream and season. Stir in the pepper flakes, if using.

Pour the sauce mixture onto the pasta mixture and stir to combine all the ingredients well. Transfer to the prepared baking dish, spread out evenly, and level the surface. Sprinkle the top with the grated cheddar, then finish with the Parmesan.

Bake in the preheated oven for about 20–30 minutes, until the top is golden and bubbling. Serve immediately with a leafy side salad.

mashed potato pie with bacon, leeks, and cheese

This is a great way to make a meal out of simple mashed potato. Bacon, leeks, and cheese make a particularly perfect trio, but you can add just about anything to this versatile dish. You should have onion at the very least, and cheese of some sort, and something green for a bit of color, after that just about anything goes!

2¼ lbs. floury potatoes, peeled

2 tablespoons olive oil

1 onion, finely chopped

2 small leeks, thinly sliced

½ cup diced thick-sliced bacon or pancetta

2 tablespoons butter

1 cup milk or light cream (or a bit of both)

1 egg, beaten

a large handful of fresh parsley leaves, chopped

a pinch of paprika

⅔ cup grated firm cheese, such as Gruyère

sea salt and freshly ground black pepper

a 10-inch round baking dish, well buttered

Serves 4–6

Halve or quarter the potatoes depending on their size; they should be about the same to cook evenly. Put them in a large saucepan, add sufficient cold water to cover, salt well, and bring to a boil. Simmer for about 20 minutes, until tender and easily pierced with a skewer.

Meanwhile, heat the oil in a skillet set over low heat. Add the onion and leeks and cook gently for about 10 minutes, until soft. Add the bacon and cook for 3–5 minutes, until just browned. Season with salt and set aside.

Preheat the oven to 375°F.

Drain the potatoes and mash coarsely, mixing in the butter and milk. Season well and add the egg. Stir to combine thoroughly.

Stir in the leek mixture, parsley, paprika, and half the cheese. Transfer to the prepared dish and spread evenly. Sprinkle over the remaining cheese and bake in the preheated oven for 35–45 minutes, until well browned. Serve immediately.

Belgian endive gratin with ham and blue cheese

This is a French recipe which traditionally calls for Gruyère cheese only, but the blue cheese used here makes it even better. There are many kinds of blue cheese and any one will do for this dish. You can also experiment with different kinds of ham; cured ham works especially well. Or, omit the ham altogether for an indulgent vegetarian supper. This is an exceptional way to prepare what is often thought of as a salad-only vegetable. Serve with lots of crusty bread or boiled potatoes and a crisp green salad.

6 Belgian endives (about 3 oz. each), rinsed and dried

1–2 tablespoons olive oil

12 thin slices smoked ham

2–3 tablespoons grated Gruyère or Parmesan

sea salt

For the sauce

3 tablespoons unsalted butter

5 tablespoons all-purpose flour

2½ cups hot milk

½ teaspoon sea salt

½ teaspoon paprika

3½ oz. grated Gruyère

2½ oz. any firm blue cheese

a 13 x 8 inch baking dish, well buttered

Serves 4–6

Preheat the oven to 400°F.

Halve the endives lengthwise. Drizzle with the oil and rub with your hands to coat evenly. Arrange in a single layer on a baking sheet. Sprinkle lightly with salt and drizzle over about 4 tablespoons water. Roast in the preheated oven for about 15 minutes, until just tender when pierced with a knife. Remove from the oven and let cool. Leave the oven on.

Meanwhile, prepare the béchamel. Melt the butter in a heavy-based saucepan. Stir in the flour and cook, stirring constantly, for 1 minute. Pour in the hot milk gradually, whisking constantly and continue whisking gently for 3–5 minutes, until the sauce begins to thicken. Season with salt and paprika and add both the cheeses. Stir well to combine.

As soon as the endives are cool enough to handle, carefully wrap each one with a slice of ham and arrange them side-by-side, seam-side down, in the prepared baking dish. Pour over the béchamel, spreading evenly to coat. Sprinkle with the grated cheese and bake in the still hot oven for about 20–30 minutes, until browned and bubbling. Serve immediately with a leafy green salad and crusty bread.

poultry

chicken tarragon bake with orzo

This recipe came into existence for a few reasons. First, chicken and tarragon are a fantastic partnership. But mostly, this is a clever use for leftover roast chicken and the accompanying vegetables, so chicken and vegetable quantities are approximate; a bit more or less is not a problem. Same for the vegetables, and you can use just about anything alongside the carrots or instead of them, green beans, peas, corn, and so on. If you are making this from scratch, steaming the chicken and carrots together is the easiest option.

2½ cups (12 oz.) shredded cooked chicken

2 carrots, quartered lengthwise, chopped and cooked

1 cup orzo (see note)

1 tablespoon olive oil

3 tablespoons fresh bread crumbs (see note on page 26)

sea salt and freshly ground black pepper

For the sauce

3 tablespoons butter

¼ cup all-purpose flour

2½ cups hot milk

½ teaspoon sea salt

1 cup chicken stock

2 teaspoons whole grain mustard

2 heaping tablespoons finely chopped fresh tarragon

a 13 x 8 inch baking dish, well buttered

Serves 4

Preheat the oven to 400°F.

First prepare the sauce. Melt the butter in a heavy-based saucepan. Stir in the flour and cook, stirring constantly, for 1 minute. Add the hot milk gradually, whisking constantly, and continue whisking gently for 3–5 minutes, until the sauce begins to thicken. Stir in the salt, stock, mustard, and tarragon and mix to combine. Taste and adjust the seasoning if necessary.

Put the chicken, carrots, and orzo in the baking dish. Add the oil, and season with salt if the chicken and vegetables are not already seasoned, and mix. Stir in the sauce and spread evenly in the prepared dish. Sprinkle the bread crumbs over the top. Cover with foil and bake in the preheated oven for 20 minutes, then remove the foil and continue baking for 20–30 minutes, until browned. Serve immediately.

Note: The Italian word orzo means barley although orzo is in fact a type of pasta. When cooked, it has a texture similar to risotto rice. Look for it in the specialty sections of supermarkets, or in Greek, Italian, and Middle Eastern markets. It can go by a variety of other names including puntaletti and romarino. If you can't find it, use another small pasta, like trofie.

chicken and spinach gratin with ricotta

A straightforward dish that's sure to be a crowd-pleaser, this is a sort of deconstructed lasagne with chicken instead of ground beef. I tend to use leftover roast chicken for this recipe which makes it quick and easy to prepare.

Put the oil in a large saucepan and set over medium heat. Add the onion and thyme and cook for 3–5 minutes, until soft. Add the garlic, pepper flakes, and parsley and cook for 1 minute. Add the wine and cook for 1 minute. Stir in the passata and sugar and season generously. Reduce the heat and simmer gently, uncovered, for 20–30 minutes.

Meanwhile, cook the macaroni according to the package instructions, drain, and set aside until needed.

Preheat the oven to 400°F.

Stir the ricotta into the tomato sauce until fully blended. Put the chicken, cooked macaroni, and spinach in a baking dish and toss well to combine. Pour over the sauce, stir well, and spread evenly in the dish. Sprinkle the cheddar and Parmesan over the top.

Bake in the preheated oven for 20–30 minutes, until golden brown. Serve immediately.

1 onion, finely chopped

2 tablespoons olive oil

1 teaspoon dried thyme

3 garlic cloves, sliced

½–1 teaspoon dried hot pepper flakes, to taste

a large handful of fresh parsley leaves, chopped

½ cup dry red or white wine

2¾ cups passata (Italian strained tomatoes) or tomato purée

a pinch of sugar

1 cup dried macaroni or other tube pasta (2 cups cooked)

1 cup (8 oz.) ricotta

1½ cups (7 oz.) shredded cooked chicken

7 oz. frozen leaf spinach, defrosted

1 cup grated mild cheddar

3 tablespoons grated Parmesan

sea salt and freshly ground black pepper

a 10-inch round baking dish

Serves 4

farmhouse chicken casserole with carrots, leeks, and potato

This is the sort of dish I make on Sunday evening to provide a meal or two during the week so I always make a big batch. But you will need a good-sized casserole dish or other lidded flameproof pot, ideally large enough to take the chicken in a single layer.

2–3 tablespoons olive oil

1 small chicken (about 1¼ lbs.), cut into pieces, plus 4 chicken thighs

1¼ lbs. carrots, peeled and sliced thickly

1 lb. trimmed leeks, cut into thick rounds

1¾ lbs. small new potatoes, cut lengthwise into wedges

a few sprigs each of fresh thyme and parsley and a bay leaf, tied firmly into a bundle with string

sea salt and freshly ground black pepper

To serve

¾ cup light cream

2 tablespoons whole grain Dijon mustard

a large handful of fresh parsley leaves, chopped

a bunch of fresh chives, snipped (optional)

a large flameproof casserole

Serves 6–8

Preheat the oven to 300°F.

Heat 2 tablespoons of the oil in a casserole dish and set over medium heat. Add the chicken pieces, skin-side down, and cook for 4–5 minutes on each side, until browned. Transfer to a dish and season generously with salt. Cover and set aside.

If there is a lot of fat in the casserole dish drain some of it off, leaving just enough to brown the vegetables. Add the carrots and leeks and cook for 5–7 minutes, stirring occasionally, until just brown. Add the potatoes and herb bundle and cook for a further 2–3 minutes. Season with salt.

Return the chicken to the casserole dish and add sufficient water just to cover. Bring to a boil, cover with a lid, and transfer to the preheated oven. Cook for about 1 hour.

Return the casserole dish to the stovetop and uncover. Using a slotted spoon, transfer the chicken and vegetables to a large serving platter. Cook the juices over medium heat for 3–5 minutes to reduce slightly, then stir in the cream. Bring to a boil, then reduce the heat and simmer gently, uncovered, for 5 minutes. Stir in the mustard, parsley, and chives and a few grinds of black pepper. Taste for seasoning and adjust as necessary. Pour the sauce over the chicken and vegetables and serve immediately.

chicken tagine with chickpeas and apricots

A tagine may sound exotic but these traditional Moroccan stews are actually very simple to prepare. The dried apricots may seem an unusual addition but they do lend a pleasant sweetness to the spices. This is best served with couscous and a small dish of harissa paste.

2 small chickens, cut into pieces

4 garlic cloves, crushed

1¼ teaspoons ground ginger

1 teaspoon coarsely ground black pepper

1 teaspoon sea salt

2 tablespoons vegetable oil

a large pinch of powdered saffron

1 teaspoon ground cinnamon

1 teaspoon ground turmeric

1 onion, grated

a handful each of chopped fresh parsley and cilantro leaves

14-oz. can chickpeas, drained

1 cup dried pitted apricots

fresh lemon wedges

couscous, to serve

harissa paste, to serve (optional)

a flameproof casserole dish

Serves 6

Place the chicken in a shallow non-metal dish and add the garlic, ginger, pepper, salt, and oil. Toss well to coat. Cover and marinate at room temperatue for at least 30 minutes, or refrigerate overnight.

Transfer the chicken and marinade to a large casserole dish. Add the saffron, cinnamon, turmeric, onion, parsley, and cilantro. Add sufficient water to just cover. Bring to a boil, then reduce the heat, cover with a lid, and simmer for 30 minutes.

Add the chickpeas and apricots, stir and adjust the seasoning. Simmer, covered, for a further 20 minutes.

Just before serving add a squeeze of fresh lemon juice and garnish each plate. Serve with couscous and a small dish of harissa paste on the side as a spicy condiment, if liked.

southwestern chicken casserole

A great weeknight supper—healthy and ready in no time. Any chicken pieces can be used, but I always have a package of chicken thighs in the freezer as back up; just remember to defrost them completely before use. Serve with rice and steamed or roasted zucchini.

8 chicken thighs, trimmed of any excess skin or fat

1 large onion, chopped

1 green bell pepper, chopped

1 tablespoon vegetable oil (optional)

2 garlic cloves, crushed

1 teaspoon ground cumin

1 teaspoon dried oregano

½ teaspoon cayenne pepper

3 fresh plum tomatoes, cored and coarsely chopped

1 tablespoon tomato paste

1⅔ cups chicken stock

1 cup corn kernels, canned or frozen

14-oz. can kidney beans, drained

2–3 tablespoons drained and chopped pickled jalapeños

a large handful of fresh cilantro leaves, chopped

sea salt and freshly ground black pepper

To serve

fresh lime wedges

4–6 chopped scallions

1 cup grated mild cheddar

1 cup sour cream

a flameproof casserole dish

Serves 4–6

Set a large casserole dish over medium heat. Add the chicken, skin-side down, and cook for 4–5 minutes on each side, until browned. Transfer to a plate and season.

Drain off most of the fat from the casserole dish, add the onion and green bell pepper and the oil only if required. Cook for about 3–5 minutes, until golden, scraping the pan to remove any cooked on chicken bits. Stir in the garlic, cumin, oregano, cayenne, and a good pinch of salt. Cook, stirring, for 1 minute more.

Add the tomatoes, tomato paste, and stock and stir well. Bring to a boil, then return the chicken to the casserole dish. Reduce the heat, cover, and simmer for about 30 minutes, until the chicken is cooked through.

Using tongs, transfer the chicken pieces to a plate. Add the corn, kidney beans, jalapeños, and cilantro to the casserole dish and mix well. Increase the heat and cook, uncovered, for 1–2 minutes, until the sauce has reduced slightly. Taste and adjust the seasoning if necessary. Return the chicken to the casserole dish.

Just before serving, squeeze over the lime juice and serve with bowls of scallions, grated cheese, and sour cream on the side.

chicken tetrazzini

The origins of this dish are unclear; is it Italian or is it American? Conventional recipes call for sherry, which I never have in my cupboard, but feel free to use some in place of the wine or balsamic vinegar if you do have some; medium dry is best. The peas are also a flourish, added for extra color and flavor. This dish comes together quickly and will be sure to please all. It is also a good way to use up chicken or even turkey.

12 oz. whole-wheat spaghetti

2–3 tablespoons olive oil

1 lb. chicken thigh meat, cut into bite-size pieces

1 small onion, halved and thinly sliced

2 tablespoons dry white wine, balsamic vinegar, or sherry

7 oz. mushrooms, thinly sliced

a large handful of fresh parsley leaves, chopped

½ cup frozen peas

4 tablespoons grated Parmesan

sea salt and freshly ground black pepper

For the sauce

3 tablespoons unsalted butter

¼ cup all-purpose flour

2 cups hot chicken stock

6 tablespoons heavy cream

a 12 x 8 inch baking dish, well buttered

Serves 4–6

Preheat the oven to 375°F.

Cook the spaghetti according to the package instructions. Drain well and toss in a little olive oil. Set aside.

Heat 1 tablespoon of the oil in a large nonstick skillet. Add the chicken pieces and onion and cook for about 5 minutes, stirring occasionally, until browned. Season well, add the wine, and cook for a further 3–5 minutes, until the liquid has almost evaporated. Transfer to a plate and set aside.

Heat the remaining 2 tablespoons of oil in the same pan. Add the mushrooms and cook for 3–5 minutes, stirring often, until just soft. Season well and stir in the parsley. Remove from the heat and set aside.

To make the sauce, melt the butter in a heavy-based saucepan set over low heat. Add the flour and cook, stirring, for 1 minute. Slowly pour in the hot stock and cream, whisking continuously, and simmer until the mixture thickens. Season to taste.

Stir in the chicken mixture, the mushrooms, and peas and mix well.

Combine the chicken mixture and cooked spaghetti in a large mixing bowl and toss to distribute the ingredients evenly. Transfer to the prepared baking dish and spread evenly. Sprinkle with Parmesan and a generous grating of black pepper. Bake in the preheated oven for 20–30 minutes, until just golden. Serve immediately.

chicken pot pie with tarragon and leeks

True confessions time: I am not confident making pies with pastry bottoms because the crust often comes out soggy. So this is a top-only pie, allowing the herb-infused sauce to shine through without any distractions. A simple mixed salad is the perfect accompaniment and makes this a wholesome family meal that's also suitable when feeding friends.

1 tablespoon olive oil

1 tablespoon butter

1 onion, chopped

2 carrots, sliced

2 trimmed leeks, sliced into ¼-inch rounds

a splash of dry white wine (optional)

2 oz. button mushrooms, quartered

1 lb. cooked chicken, cut into bite-size pieces

½ cup frozen peas

13-oz. package puff pastry, defrosted if frozen

a little beaten egg, for glazing

sea salt and freshly ground black pepper

For the sauce

3 tablespoons butter

⅓ cup all-purpose flour

1 cup hot chicken stock

6 tablespoons light cream

several sprigs of fresh tarragon, leaves stripped and chopped

a small bunch of fresh chives, snipped

leaves from a small bunch of fresh parsley, finely chopped

a 12 x 8 inch baking dish

Serves 4–6

Preheat the oven to 375°F.

Heat the oil and butter in a large nonstick skillet. Add the onion, carrots, and leeks and cook, stirring, for 5–8 minutes, until soft. Season well with salt and pepper, add the mushrooms and wine, if using, and cook for 3–5 minutes more. You may need to add a drop more oil or butter. Add the chicken and peas, and set aside.

To make the sauce, melt the butter in a heavy-based saucepan set over low heat. Add the flour and cook for 1 minute, stirring continuously. Slowly pour in the hot stock and cream, whisking continuously, and simmer until the mixture thickens. Season well. Stir in the tarragon, chives, and parsley. Taste and adjust the seasoning if necessary.

Transfer the chicken mixture to the baking dish and pour over the sauce. Mix to combine.

Roll out the pastry on a lightly floured surface. Lay the sheet on top of the filling, crimping the edges to sit just inside the edge and trimming off any excess with a sharp knife (you can use the trimmings for decoration, if liked.) Cut an "X" in the middle to allow steam to escape and brush with the beaten egg. Bake in the preheated oven for 30–40 minutes, until golden brown. Serve immediately.

Variation: For a vegetarian version, omit the chicken and use vegetable stock. Increase the carrot, leek, and mushroom quantities slightly and add about 10 oz. of any one or a combination of the following vegetables which has been cooked and cubed where appropriate: rutabaga, turnip, parsnip, broccoli and/or cauliflower florets, zucchini, green beans, or asparagus.

braised duck and white bean cassoulet

The idea of long-simmered duck in a garlicky sauce is always appetizing, but not always easy to achieve due to time constraints. This is shortcut cassoulet, but cassoulet in spirit because it combines duck with bacon and a browned topping of white beans. It's a good dish for cold weather and easy to prepare in advance. Simply add a mixed green salad and crusty bread for a substantial and satisfying meal that's great for entertaining.

4 duck legs (about 14 oz. each)

2 onions, halved and sliced

1 large carrot, diced

5 oz. pancetta or lardons, diced

1 teaspoon dried thyme

4 garlic cloves, sliced

1 cup dry white wine

2 x 14-oz. cans chopped tomatoes

1 cup pitted green olives

1 bay leaf

2 x 14-oz. cans haricot or cannellini beans, drained

1 cup bread crumbs (see note on page 26)

sea salt and freshly ground black pepper

a 13 x 9 inch baking dish

Serves 4–6

Preheat the oven to 325°F.

Arrange the duck legs skin-side down in a large saucepan and cook over medium heat for 4–5 minutes on each side, until browned. Transfer to a plate, sprinkle with salt.

Drain off all but 1 tablespoon of fat from the pan. Add the onions and carrots and cook for about 5 minutes, until soft. Add the pancetta and thyme and cook for a further 3–4 minutes. Add the garlic and cook for 1 minute. Season and add the wine. Bring to a boil and boil, uncovered, for 1 minute. Add the tomatoes, olives, and bay leaf. Reduce the heat and simmer, uncovered, for 5 minutes. Taste and adjust the seasoning if necessary.

Using tongs, transfer the duck legs to the baking dish. Pour over the sauce and spread evenly. If necessary, add sufficient water to submerge the duck by about 1 inch. Cover tightly with foil and transfer to the preheated oven to cook for 1½ hours. Check after 1 hour. (The recipe can be prepared up to 24 hours in advance up to this point. Cover and refrigerate until needed.)

Remove the baking dish from the oven and increase the heat to 400°F.

Add the beans to the dish in an even layer, sprinkle the bread crumbs over the top and season well. Return to the oven and bake for 20–25 minutes more, until well browned on top. Serve immediately.

chicken and sweet potato pie

Americans tend to eat sweet potatoes and stuffing mainly around holiday season festivities. This recipe is designed to make it taste like Christmas any time. It is also designed as a way to recycle leftover roast chicken but you could be forgiven for buying a rotisserie chicken expressly for this dish. To obtain the stale bread, I use the end pieces from sliced loaves that never seem to get eaten, and toast them in the oven, alongside the sweet potatoes. This is a meal in a single dish, requiring only a green salad and good appetites.

3½ lbs. sweet potatoes, peeled and cut into chunks

3–4 tablespoons olive oil

2–4 tablespoons butter

1 onion, diced

4 oz. thick-sliced bacon, chopped

2 cups chopped mushrooms

2 celery ribs, chopped

2 garlic cloves, crushed

2 teaspoons dried thyme

2½–3½ oz. cooked sausage, chopped

¾ cup vacuum-packed peeled chestnuts, chopped

a large handful of fresh parsley leaves, chopped

½ a chicken (about 1½ lbs.), cooked and meat shredded

4 oz. stale or toasted bread, broken into small pieces

5 tablespoons milk

¾ cup chicken stock or water

sea salt and freshly ground black pepper

a 10–12 inch round baking dish, well buttered

Serves 4–6

Preheat the oven to 425°F.

Toss the sweet potatoes with the olive oil and arrange in a single layer on a baking sheet. Roast in the preheated oven for about 45 minutes, until tender and browned. Reduce the oven temperature to 400°F. Let the sweet potatoes cool, then peel, mash with butter to taste and season with salt. Set aside.

Heat some of the oil in a skillet. Add the onion and cook for 2–3 minutes, until soft. Season with salt, then add the bacon, mushrooms, and celery and cook for 3–5 minutes, stirring often. Add the garlic, thyme, sausage, and chestnuts and cook for about 1 minute. Stir in the parsley and chicken and set aside.

In a bowl, combine the bread pieces and milk and toss to coat. The bread should be moist, you may need to add more milk. Add the bread to the chicken mixture, along with the stock. Stir well. Taste and adjust the seasoning.

Spread the chicken mixture in an even layer in the prepared baking dish. It will dry out slightly with baking, so if it seems dry at the outset, add a bit more of any liquid: stock, milk, or water. Top with the mashed sweet potato, spread evenly. Bake in the preheated oven for about 45 minutes. (The sweet potato won't brown but should start to blacken slightly where peaked.)

chicken meatballs with roasted onions and tomatoes

Not your average meatball, these rarely come out perfectly round but their imperfection is part of their charm. An unusual meatball requires something more exotic than just tomato sauce, hence the roasted tomatoes and onions, which works perfectly.

Preheat the oven to 400°F.

Halve 1 of the onions and chop coarsely; set aside. Cut the remaining onions into quarters and toss with 2–3 tablespoons of the oil and the thyme. Arrange on the foil-lined baking sheet with the tomatoes. Set aside while you prepare the meatballs.

In a small food processor combine the coarsely chopped onion, mushrooms, pancetta, and parsley. Process until finely chopped. Transfer to a skillet and add 1–2 tablespoons of the oil. Cook for 3–5 minutes, until softened. Add the garlic, season well, and cook for 1 minute more. Let cool slightly.

In a bowl, combine the chicken, paprika, egg, bread crumbs, and the cooled mushroom mixture. Add a good pinch of salt. Mix well with your hands to combine. Take a small pinch of the mixture and cook it in the pan used to cook the mushroom mixture. When cooked, taste it and adjust the seasoning as necessary. The mixture should be quite moist and it will be possible—if difficult—to form the mixture into balls. If it is too dry, soften with milk, adding 1 tablespoon at a time.

Form the chicken mixture into roughly shaped meatballs, about the size of a large walnut, and arrange on the paper-lined baking sheet. Season the onions and tomatoes and put both of the sheets into the preheated oven. Bake for about 35–45 minutes, until the meatballs and vegetables are browned. Serve together.

Note: If you have space, 2 sheets can fit alongside one another in extra wide ovens. But do not place 1 sheet on a shelf above the other as the contents of the bottom sheet will not brown properly. If this is a problem, best to roast the vegetables first, then set aside while roasting the meatballs and reheat just before serving.

3 onions

6 fresh plum tomatoes, cored and quartered

4 tablespoons olive oil

1 teaspoon dried thyme

4 oz. mushrooms, coarsely chopped

4 oz. pancetta or ham

a large handful of fresh parsley leaves, chopped

2 garlic cloves, crushed

1 lb. ground chicken

1 teaspoon paprika

1 egg, beaten

5 tablespoons fresh bread crumbs (see note on page 26)

milk, to soften

sea salt and freshly ground black pepper

2 baking sheets, 1 lined with foil the other with baking parchment

Serves 4–6

Spanish-style chicken and rice

This is really a cheat's paella, but it tastes just as good as the real thing. The shortcut here is the oven baking; easier than stirring and watching over the stovetop like a hawk. It's a meal in itself, but a nice bottle of Spanish red and some crusty bread would not go amiss.

1 tablespoon olive oil

8 chicken thighs, trimmed of excess skin and fat

1 onion, diced

1 orange or yellow bell pepper, seeded and diced

1 carrot, peeled and diced

4 garlic cloves, crushed

½ teaspoon Spanish smoked sweet paprika (pimentón dulce)

2 cups paella rice

6–8 cooking chorizo (about 8 oz.), cut into large pieces

½ cup dry white wine

1¼ cups chicken stock

14-oz. can chopped tomatoes

1 bay leaf

2 cups frozen peas

a large handful of fresh flat-leaf parsley leaves, chopped

sea salt and freshly ground black pepper

a flameproof casserole dish

Serves 4

Preheat the oven to 400°F.

Heat the oil in a casserole dish. Add the chicken thighs, skin-side down, and cook for 3–5 minutes on each side, until browned. Transfer to a plate and season with salt.

Add the onion, bell pepper, and carrot to the casserole dish and cook for 2–3 minutes. Add the garlic, paprika, rice, and chorizo and continue cooking, stirring to coat the rice in oil, for about 1 minute more.

Stir in the wine, stock, and tomatoes, add the bay leaf and season well. Return the chicken to the casserole dish. Cover with a lid and transfer to the preheated oven. Cook for 20 minutes. Remove the casserole from the oven and stir in the peas. Return to the oven and cook for a further 10 minutes, until the rice is tender. (If it seems dry when adding the peas, add a splash of water.)

Remove from the oven and let stand, covered, for about 10 minutes. Remove the bay leaf, stir in the parsley, fluff up the rice with a fork, and serve.

Moroccan chicken phyllo pie

Ideal for large gatherings or buffets, this is best when made in advance giving the flavors time to mingle. The filling can also be made into individual pies. Serve with a grated carrot salad dressed with orange juice and olive oil, and couscous with chickpeas.

2 tablespoons olive oil

1 onion, grated

1 teaspoon ground cinnamon

2 teaspoons ground ginger

½ teaspoon turmeric

a pinch of saffron threads

1 teaspoon paprika

½ teaspoon ground cumin

½ teaspoon ground black pepper

1 garlic clove, crushed

8 chicken thighs, skin removed

½ cup raisins

½ cup slivered almonds

a large handful of fresh cilantro leaves, chopped

1 tablespoon freshly squeezed lemon juice

9-oz. package phyllo pastry, defrosted if frozen

2–3 tablespoons butter, melted

sea salt and freshly ground black pepper

a 10-inch round baking dish or pie plate, well buttered

Serves 4–6

Heat the oil in a large saucepan set over low heat. Add the onion and cook for 5–8 minutes, until just soft. Stir in the spices and garlic and cook for 1 minute. Add the chicken and stir to coat in the spiced oil. Add ¾ cup water and the raisins. Season generously with salt. Bring to a boil, reduce the heat, cover, and simmer for about 20–30 minutes, until the chicken is cooked through. Set aside.

Preheat the oven to 375°F.

When the chicken is cool enough to handle, shred the meat and discard the bones. Return the meat to the cooking juices. Mix well, taste, and adjust the seasoning. The mixture should be very moist but it should not be soupy. If there is a lot of liquid, return to the heat and cook to reduce slightly. Stir in the almonds, cilantro, and lemon juice. Set aside.

To assemble, place 2 sheets of phyllo on the work surface. Using the baking dish as a template, cut out 2 circles of phyllo to fit. Cover with a clean, damp kitchen towel and set aside. Line the sides of the dish with the remaining phyllo sheets, positioning each one with an overhang and not quite reaching the middle. Continue until the edge is covered with overhanging sheets of phyllo. Brush the bottom of the dish with melted butter and top with one of the phyllo circles. Brush with butter and top with the remaining circle.

Transfer the chicken mixture to the phyllo-lined dish, spreading it evenly. Fold in the overhanging phyllo to part-enclose the filling, crinkling it as you go. Brush with melted butter.

Bake in the preheated oven for 30–40 minutes, until just golden. Serve warm or at room temperature.

ginger and star anise braised chicken

A wonderfully simple and healthy way to enjoy chicken that will also fill your kitchen with exotic aromas. This is a real crowd pleaser and it gets better over time so it is worthwhile preparing in advance, or making a big batch to ensure leftovers. To do this, use two small chickens, or 1 medium and a package of chicken pieces, such as thighs, and double all the other ingredients. This also works very well with chicken wings as party food. To serve for dinner, accompany with steamed or sautéed snow peas and boiled rice.

1 tablespoon vegetable oil

1 medium chicken (2 lbs.), cut into serving pieces

1-inch piece of fresh ginger, peeled and cut into thin strips

3 garlic cloves, sliced

⅓ cup Chinese rice wine

½ cup chicken stock or water

1 tablespoon runny honey

1 star anise

¼ cup light soy sauce

freshly squeezed juice of 1 clementine (or 3–4 tablespoons fresh orange juice)

2 scallions, thinly sliced

rice, to serve

sea salt

Serves 4

Heat the oil in a large saucepan. When hot, add the chicken pieces, skin-side down, and cook for about 4–5 minutes on each side, until browned. Transfer to a plate, season lightly with salt and set aside.

Drain all but 1 tablespoon of fat from the pan. Add the ginger, garlic, rice wine, stock, honey, star anise, and soy sauce and bring to a boil. Add the clementine juice and the chicken. Reduce the heat, cover, and simmer gently for 15 minutes. Turn the chicken pieces and simmer for about 15 minutes more, until cooked through. Taste and adjust the seasoning if necessary.

Remove the chicken from the pan with a slotted spoon and set aside. Bring the liquid back to a boil and cook for 2–3 minutes to reduce slightly. Remove the star anise, return the chicken the pan and stir to coat in the sauce. Sprinkle with the scallions and serve with rice and snow peas, if liked.

spicy chicken casserole with sweet peppers

Colorful with fantastic flavors, this recipe is one I come back to time and time again. The bell pepper mixture is inspired by a traditional French Basque country recipe for piperade, which is usually made to accompany grilled tuna steaks and sometimes scrambled eggs. Rice makes a nice accompaniment, as does a simple green salad.

2 tablespoons olive oil

1 large chicken (about 4½ lbs.), cut into 8 pieces

2 onions halved and sliced

2 red bell peppers, halved, seeded, and sliced

2 yellow bell peppers, halved, seeded, and sliced

4 garlic cloves, crushed

2 fresh green chiles, thinly sliced

¼ teaspoon cayenne pepper (optional)

½ cup dry white wine

14-oz. can chopped tomatoes

a large handful of fresh parsley leaves, chopped

a pinch of sugar

sea salt and freshly ground black pepper

rice, to serve

Serves 4

Heat the oil in a large skillet set over medium heat. Add the chicken pieces skin-side down and cook for 5–10 minutes on each side, until browned. Transfer the chicken to a plate, season with salt and set aside.

Add the onions and bell peppers to the pan, season and cook for 10–15 minutes, stirring occasionally, until soft. Stir in the garlic and chiles and cook for 1 minute. If you want this really hot, add the cayenne. Add the wine and cook for 3–5 minutes, until most of the liquid has reduced. Stir in the tomatoes, parsley, and sugar. Taste and adjust the seasoning as necessary. Return the chicken to the pan and bury in the sauce.

Reduce the heat, cover, and simmer for 30–40 minutes, until the chicken is tender and cooked through. Serve immediately with rice.

coconut chicken curry with spiced lentil dhal and potatoes

3 tablespoons vegetable oil

1 lb. boneless chicken, cut into bite-size pieces

3 tablespoons garam masala

¾ cup coconut milk

3 tablespoons cumin seeds

2 tablespoons black mustard seeds

1 onion, finely chopped

1½-inch piece of fresh ginger, peeled and grated

3 garlic cloves, crushed

1 fresh red chile, chopped

3 teaspoons ground cumin

1 teaspoon ground turmeric

¼–1 teaspoon cayenne pepper, to taste

1 tablespoon tomato purée

2 cups chicken stock

1 cinnamon stick

1¼ cups split red lentils

12 oz. new potatoes, scrubbed or peeled and cubed

1 cup frozen peas

1 tablespoon runny honey

freshly squeezed juice of 1 lemon

sea salt

a handful of fresh cilantro leaves, to serve

rice and/or warmed naan bread, to serve

Serves 6–8

This is a long list of ingredients, but the dish comes together very quickly so don't let it put you off. As with most highly spiced dishes, this benefits from being made in advance, to allow the spices time to mingle, but it's still flavorful enough to stand up to a last minute whim for immediate consumption. Serve with rice and warmed naan bread.

Heat 1 tablespoon of the oil in a large skillet set over medium heat. Add the chicken and 2 tablespoons of the garam masala and season well with salt. Cook for 3–5 minutes, stirring, until golden. Add the coconut milk and simmer for about 10 minutes, until the chicken is cooked. Set aside.

Heat the remaining oil in a large saucepan. Add the cumin and mustard seeds and cook until they begin to sputter. Stir in the onion, ginger, garlic, chile, cumin, turmeric, cayenne, tomato paste, and remaining garam masala and cook, stirring, for 1–2 minutes.

Add the stock, ¾ cup water, cinnamon, lentils, and potatoes and mix well. Reduce the heat and simmer, uncovered, for 35–45 minutes, until the potatoes are tender. Check often and top up with water if required; the mixture should be liquid but not overly soupy. Taste and adjust the seasoning if necessary. Stir in the honey and lemon juice.

Stir the chicken mixture into the lentil mixture. Add the peas and simmer for 5 minutes more. Sprinkle with cilantro and serve with rice and warmed naan bread.

Variation: For a vegetarian version, replace the chicken with 1 lb. blanched cauliflower florets, and simmer in the coconut milk until tender, before adding to the lentils.

fish and shellfish

smoked haddock and potato gratin

This may sound and look rustic but the taste is very sophisticated, making it an ideal choice for when you need to cook something elegant yet easy. Use good-quality undyed smoked haddock fillet for this dish—smoked trout or smoked Alaskan sable are suitable substitutes if haddock is unavailable. Serve the gratin with sautéed haricots verts or, if you are serving it as a midweek dinner, then a simple green salad alongside is all that's required.

3½ lbs. waxy potatoes, peeled

1 bay leaf

½ oz. dried wild mushrooms

1 onion, chopped

2 tablespoons olive oil

2 cups sliced white mushrooms

½ cup dry white wine

9–10 oz. undyed smoked haddock fillet, shredded, bones removed

a large handful of fresh flat-leaf parsley leaves, chopped

1½ cups light cream

1 cup milk

2 tablespoons butter, melted

sea salt and freshly ground black pepper

a 13 x 8 inch baking dish, well buttered

Serves 4–6

Put the potatoes in a large saucepan, add the bay leaf and sufficient cold water to cover well. Boil until almost tender when pierced with a knife. Drain. When cool enough to handle slice into ¼-inch thick rounds.

Put the dried mushrooms in a heatproof bowl and add sufficient boiling water to cover. Soak for about 15 minutes, until soft. Discard all but 2 tablespoons of the soaking liquid. Drain the mushrooms, chop coarsely, and set aside.

Preheat the oven to 400°F.

Put 1 tablespoon of the oil in a large skillet and add the onion. Cook for 3–5 minutes, until soft. Add the white mushrooms and the remaining oil and season well. Cook, stirring, for 3–5 minutes, until the mushrooms begin to brown. Add the wine and reserved mushroom soaking liquid and cook for 1 minute. Stir in the dried mushrooms, haddock, and parsley and cook for 2–3 minutes.

Combine the cream and milk. Season and set aside.

To assemble, arrange half the potato slices on the bottom of the prepared baking dish (save the most even and attractive slices for the top layer.) Sprinkle lightly with salt. Spread the fish mixture in an even layer on top of the potatoes. Top with the remaining potatoes, arranged neatly. Sprinkle lightly with salt, then pour over the cream mixture. Brush the top with melted butter and bake in the preheated oven for about 1–1½ hours, until golden. Serve immediately.

crispy-crumbed fish bake with mushrooms and tomato

Easy, healthy, and full of flavor, this recipe will put a nutritious supper on the table in under an hour. Because there is very little sauce, this goes well with spinach tagliatelle tossed in a bit of cream but it can just as easily be served with plain boiled rice. Accompany with any green side vegetable, such as broccoli or haricots verts.

1 cup fresh bread crumbs (see note on page 26)

½ teaspoon paprika

1 heaping tablespoon finely grated cheddar

1¼ lbs. boneless, skinless fish fillets, such as hake or pollock, cut into bite-size pieces

4 fresh plum tomatoes, cored and very thinly sliced

10 oz. button mushrooms, trimmed and thinly sliced

3 tablespoons dry white wine

3–4 tablespoons butter, cut into small pieces

leaves from a small bunch of fresh parsley, chopped

sea salt and freshly ground black pepper

a 13 x 8 inch baking dish, very well buttered

Serves 4

Preheat the oven to 375°F.

In a small bowl, mix the bread crumbs with the paprika and season well. Mix in the cheese. Set aside.

Arrange the fish in the prepared baking dish and season well. Arrange an even layer of tomato slices on top and sprinkle lightly with salt. Top with an even layer of mushroom slices. Pour over the wine. Dot the top with butter and sprinkle over the parsley. Sprinkle over the seasoned bread crumbs in an even layer.

Bake in the preheated oven for 30–40 minutes, until browned and the fish is cooked through. Check after 20 minutes; if the top browns too quickly, cover loosely with foil and continue cooking.

After about 30 minutes cooking time, remove the foil (if using), increase the heat to 425°F and cook for 3–5 minutes more, just to crisp and brown the top nicely. Serve immediately.

fish pie with leeks and herbs

A classic British dish, made slightly more stylish here by the addition of leeks and fresh herbs. It is important to use a mixture of different fish, as this gives the dish a more interesting taste and texture, but if smoked fish is difficult to obtain, simply increase the quantity of the others. Serve with peas or wilted fresh spinach.

2¼ lbs. floury potatoes, peeled

2 bay leaves

1 stick unsalted butter

about 3⅓ cups milk (1 cup of which is warmed)

1 tablespoon olive oil

1 trimmed leek, cut into thin rounds

2 tablespoons dry white wine

10 oz. any firm white fish fillet, such as cod

7 oz. boneless, skinless salmon

6 oz. undyed smoked haddock

6 oz. peeled cooked shrimp

⅓ cup all-purpose flour

1 teaspoon dry mustard powder

a small bunch of chives, snipped

a large handful of fresh parsley leaves, chopped

sea salt and freshly ground black pepper

a 12 x 8 inch baking dish, well buttered

Serves 6

Put the potatoes in a large saucepan and add sufficient cold water to cover. Add 1 of the bay leaves, season with salt, and bring to a boil. Cook until the potatoes are tender when pierced with a knife. Drain well. Working in batches, mash the potatoes with all but 3 tablespoons of the butter, the 1 cup warmed milk, and some salt. Repeat until all the potatoes are mashed. Taste and adjust the seasoning. The mixture should be slightly thinner than ordinary mash to allow for baking. Set aside.

Preheat the oven to 375°F.

Put the oil in a small saucepan and add the leek. Cook for about 5 minutes, until soft. Season lightly, add the wine, and cook until the liquid is almost fully reduced. Set aside.

Combine the remaining milk and bay leaf in a large shallow pan and bring to a boil. Add the white fish and poach for about 5 minutes, until almost cooked. Transfer to a plate with a slotted spoon and season lightly. Add the salmon and repeat. Add the smoked haddock and repeat. Measure the poaching milk; if it is not quite 2½ cups, top it up with more milk.

Melt the remaining butter in a medium saucepan set over low heat. Add the flour and cook, whisking, for 1 minute. Slowly pour in the reserved milk, whisking continuously, and simmer until the mixture thickens. Add the mustard and season to taste. Stir in the chives and parsley.

Break the fish into pieces and put in the prepared dish. Add the shrimp and leeks. Pour over the sauce and stir well to mix. Spread evenly. Top with the mash and spread in an even layer.

Bake in the preheated oven for 35–45 minutes, until browned and bubbling up around the edges. Serve immediately.

fish in veracruz sauce

A feisty, fiery sauce that is a cinch to prepare. This recipe can easily be doubled for a crowd, or halved for two. Serve with rice, warmed soft flour tortillas, and avocado slices. This recipe works equally well with other seafood, such as scallops or jumbo shrimp.

4 fish fillets (1½–2 lbs.), such as sea bass, hake, or red snapper

freshly squeezed juice of 2 limes

3 tablespoons olive oil

1 large onion, finely chopped

4 garlic cloves, crushed

2 x 14-oz. cans chopped tomatoes

½ cup pitted green olives, sliced

2 tablespoons drained capers (optional)

2–3 tablespoons sliced pickled jalapeños with their juice

3 tablespoons finely chopped fresh flat-leaf parsley leaves

½ teaspoon dried oregano

2 fresh bay leaves

a large handful of fresh cilantro leaves, chopped

sea salt and freshly ground black pepper

To serve

rice

warmed flour tortillas

2 ripe avocados, pitted and sliced

lime wedges

Serves 4

Put the fish in a nonreactive dish and pour over the lime juice. Sprinkle with salt, turn with your hands to coat, then cover and marinate while you prepare the sauce. (You can also prepare the fish up to several hours in advance, keep in the refrigerator until needed.)

Heat the oil in a skillet large enough to hold all the fish in a single layer. Add the onion and cook over low heat for 5–10 minutes, until soft. Season with salt, add the garlic, and cook for 1 minute more.

Add the tomatoes, olives, capers (if using), jalapeños, parsley, oregano, and bay leaves. Season, stir to mix and simmer gently for 15 minutes. Taste and adjust the seasoning if necessary.

Add the fish to the pan along with the lime juice marinade, burying the fillets in the sauce. Cover and cook for 3–5 minutes. Turn and continue cooking for 3–5 minutes more, until the fish is opaque and cooked through. Discard the bay leaves and serve immediately with rice, warmed tortillas, and slices of avocado.

tuna pasta puttanesca

This dish comes together quickly but always tastes better the next day so make it ahead of time if you can, or make extra to enjoy as leftovers. This is best served with a crisp green salad, crusty bread, and a bottle of hearty Italian red wine.

2 tablespoons olive oil

1 onion, finely chopped

1 teaspoon dried oregano

4 garlic cloves, sliced

a large handful of fresh flat-leaf parsley leaves, chopped

½–1 teaspoon dried hot pepper flakes, to taste

½ cup dry white or red wine

2¾ cups passata (Italian strained tomatoes) or tomato purée

a pinch of sugar

10 oz. dried fusilli

½ cup pitted black olives, sliced

1 tablespoon drained capers

4 anchovy fillets in oil, chopped

12-oz. can tuna in oil, drained and flaked

3 tablespoons grated Parmesan

sea salt and freshly ground black pepper

a 13 x 9 inch baking dish

Serves 4

Heat the oil in a large saucepan set over medium heat and add the onion and oregano. Cook for 3–5 minutes, stirring, until soft. Add the garlic, parsley, and pepper flakes and cook for 1 minute. Add the wine and cook for 1 minute. Stir in the passata and sugar and season well. Reduce the heat and simmer gently, uncovered, for 20–30 minutes.

Meanwhile, cook the pasta according to the package instructions. Drain, toss in a little oil, and set aside.

Preheat the oven to 400°F.

Stir the olives, capers, anchovies, and tuna into the sauce. Taste and adjust the seasoning if necessary. Add the cooked pasta and stir well to combine.

Transfer to a baking dish and spread evenly. Sprinkle the Parmesan over the top and bake in the preheated oven for 20–30 minutes, until golden. Serve immediately.

Burmese fish curry

This is a quick and zesty curry, made fragrant with fresh tomatoes and ginger, which offers a welcome change from the creamy coconut variety. Make this as spicy as you like by adjusting the quantity of chiles. It tastes best when assembled at the last minute to keep the flavors fresh and it also works well with shrimp. Serve with basmati rice.

1 large onion, coarsely chopped

2 tablespoons vegetable oil

¼–½ teaspoon dried hot pepper flakes

4 garlic cloves, crushed

3 fresh plum tomatoes, cored and chopped

2-inch piece of fresh ginger, peeled and grated

1 teaspoon paprika

½ teaspoon turmeric

1 lb. white fish fillets, such as hake or pollock, cut into pieces

1–2 fresh green chiles, diced

1–2 tablespoons Thai fish sauce

a large handful of fresh cilantro leaves, chopped

sea salt

basmati rice, to serve

lemon wedges, to serve

Serves 4

Put the onions in a small food processor and blend until very finely chopped. Heat the oil in a large, deep-sided skillet set over low heat. Add the onion and cook for 3–5 minutes, until just soft. Add the pepper flakes, garlic, tomatoes, ginger, paprika, turmeric, and a little salt. Simmer uncovered for 5 minutes, stirring often.

Add the fish, chiles, and 1 tablespoon of the fish sauce to the pan. Add sufficient water to obtain a liquid sauce; it should be thick and soupy.

Cover and cook over low heat for 7–8 minutes, until the fish is cooked through. Taste and add more fish sauce if required. Sprinkle over the cilantro just before serving. Spoon over rice and arrange the lemon wedges on the side for squeezing.

Moroccan fish tagine

This recipe uses an ordinary baking dish, with foil in place of the conical tagine lid. Not authentic, but an acceptable replacement. Another slight modification is the use of fillets because it is more traditional to use whole fish, such as sea bass. But the herbs and spices are based on a traditional Moroccan recipe and the taste is fabulously genuine. Serve with couscous or rice, as preferred.

Combine the cilantro, salt, garlic, paprika, cayenne, cumin, lemon juice, and olive oil in a shallow baking dish (not metal) large enough to hold the fish in a single layer. Mix well. Add the fish, and use your hands to turn the pieces until they are coated in the oil. Cover with plastic wrap and refrigerate while you prepare the sauce (at least 30 minutes and up to several hours.)

Preheat the oven to 375°F.

To make the sauce, put the onion, parsley, and garlic in a food processor and process until finely chopped. Transfer to a saucepan set over medium heat. Add the tomatoes, 1¼ cups water, carrots, cumin, cayenne, and sugar. Season and stir to blend. Bring to a boil, then reduce the heat and simmer, covered, for about 15 minutes, until the carrots are tender.

Remove the fish from the refrigerator. Transfer it to a plate and pour the tomato sauce into the ovenproof dish containing the marinade and mix well. Return the fish to the dish, arranging it on top of the sauce. Cover with foil and bake in the preheated oven for 10–20 minutes, until the fish is cooked through.

Remove from the oven, sprinkle with the cilantro sprigs and grind over some black pepper. Serve with the lemon wedges on the side for squeezing and couscous or rice, as preferred.

1¼ lbs. boneless, skinless white fish fillet

1 onion, coarsely chopped

a handful of fresh parsley leaves

2 garlic cloves, crushed

14-oz. can chopped tomatoes

4 thin carrots, halved and sliced

1 teaspoon ground cumin

½ teaspoon cayenne pepper

a pinch of sugar

sea salt and freshly ground black pepper

lemon wedges, to serve

couscous or rice, to serve

For the marinade

2 tablespoons chopped fresh cilantro leaves

1 tablespoon coarse sea salt

4 garlic cloves, crushed

2 tablespoons paprika

½ teaspoon cayenne pepper

1 tablespoon ground cumin

freshly squeezed juice of ½ a lemon

½ cup olive oil

a baking dish, large enough to take the fish in a single layer

Serves 4

roasted Provençal salmon and vegetables with rouille

Bright and festive, the colors and aromas in this dish will transport you to the south of France. Be sure to choose a wrinkly, gutsy black olive for this dish; ordinary pitted black olives simply won't do. This is ideal for both informal dining or entertaining and in either case you can serve it straight from the roasting pan. Accompany with crusty bread and a green salad lightly dressed with extra virgin olive oil, good quality wine vinegar, and lots of fresh herbs.

1 lb. baby new potatoes, scrubbed and quartered

1 lb. zucchini, halved and quartered

1 fennel bulb, halved and sliced

1 red bell pepper, cored, seeded, and sliced

1 yellow bell pepper, cored, seeded, and sliced

3 fresh plum tomatoes, cored and quartered

2 red onions, sliced into sixths

a good pinch of saffron threads

a few sprigs of fresh thyme

4–5 tablespoons olive oil

1 cup pitted black olives, halved

a small handful of fresh basil leaves, shredded

4 boneless, skinless salmon fillets (about 5 oz. each)

sea salt and freshly ground black pepper

For the rouille

¾ cup fresh mayonnaise

2–4 garlic cloves, crushed

½ teaspoon paprika

a pinch of cayenne pepper

Serves 4

Preheat the oven to 425°F.

Combine all of the vegetables in a large roasting pan. Add the saffron and thyme and a good dose of the olive oil. Toss with your hands to coat evenly. Spread the vegetables out in an even layer and sprinkle with salt.

Bake in the preheated oven for 25–30 minutes, until just browned.

Meanwhile, prepare the rouille. Combine all the ingredients in a small bowl, adding garlic and cayenne to taste. Mix well, adjust the seasoning and set aside.

Remove the vegetables from the oven and sprinkle over the olives and basil. Arrange the salmon on top, drizzle a little of the olive oil over each fillet, and season with salt and pepper. Return to the oven and bake for about 15 minutes more, until the salmon is just cooked through. Serve immediately, with the rouille on the side for spooning.

salmon, broccoli, and potato gratin with pesto

This can be prepared the night or morning before serving. Simply assemble the gratin, up to the point of pouring on the cream, cover, and refrigerate. I never use green basil pesto from a jar as it cannot compare to real pesto. If you can't get fresh pesto then it's better to replace it in this recipe with some chopped fresh parsley, lots of freshly ground black pepper, and 1 tablespoon of grated lemon peel. A different taste, equally nice and an honest one.

2 lbs. waxy potatoes, peeled

a large head of broccoli (about 1 lb.), separated into florets

14 oz. boneless, skinless salmon fillet

1 tablespoon olive oil

3 tablespoons fresh bread crumbs (see note on page 26)

4 tablespoons grated Parmesan

1 cup light cream

2 tablespoons fresh pesto

4 tablespoons milk

2–3 tablespoons butter, cut into small pieces

sea salt and freshly ground black pepper

a 12 x 8 inch baking dish, well buttered

Serves 4–6

Preheat the oven to 400°F.

Put the potatoes in a large saucepan and add sufficient cold water to cover. Boil until almost tender when pierced with a knife. Drain. When cool enough to handle slice into ⅛-inch thick rounds.

Bring another saucepan of water to a boil. Add the broccoli and a pinch of salt and cook for 3–4 minutes, until just tender. Drain and let cool. Cut into bite-size pieces and set aside.

Rub the salmon fillets with the oil and place on a piece of foil, turned up at the sides to catch any juices, and put it on a baking sheet. Sprinkle with a little salt. Bake in the preheated oven for about 10–15 minutes, until cooked through. Let cool, then flake, removing any small bones and set aside.

In a small bowl, mix together the bread crumbs and 2 tablespoons of the Parmesan. Season well and set aside. In another bowl, stir together the cream and pesto. Season well and set aside.

To assemble, arrange the potato slices on the bottom of the prepared baking dish in an even layer, sprinkle with salt, the remaining Parmesan, and drizzle with the milk. Arrange the broccoli in an even layer on top of the potatoes and season lightly. Top with the cooked salmon in an even layer.

Pour over the pesto and cream mixture. Sprinkle the bread crumb mixture over the top and dot with butter. Bake in the preheated oven for 25–30 minutes, until just browned and crisp on top. Serve immediately.

tuna noodle casserole

In my childhood, this would have been made with cream of mushroom soup from a can. And the crispy topping could have included crushed potato chips, depending on the whim of the cook. Given that list of ingredients, it's hard to imagine that anyone has fond nostalgia for this dish, but it is one of those childhood favorites among Americans of a certain generation. Here, it is brought up to date with a freshly-made white sauce, mushrooms, and capers, if you like. Serve with a generous and colorful mixed salad.

2 tablespoons olive oil

3 scallions, thinly sliced

1 celery rib, finely chopped

4 oz. button mushrooms, halved and thinly sliced

2 tablespoons capers (optional)

1½ cups fresh bread crumbs (see note on page 26)

a good pinch of paprika

12 oz. dried egg tagliatelle

3 tablespoons unsalted butter

⅓ cup all-purpose flour

2½ cups hot milk

1 teaspoon mustard powder

12-oz. can tuna in oil, drained and flaked

a large handful of fresh parsley leaves, chopped

sea salt and freshly ground black pepper

a 12 x 8 inch baking dish, well buttered

Serves 4

Preheat the oven to 350°F.

Heat the oil in a large skillet and add the scallions, celery, and mushrooms. Cook over medium heat for 3–5 minutes, until soft. Season lightly with salt, stir in the capers (if using), and set aside. Season the bread crumbs and add the paprika. Set aside.

Cook the pasta according to the package instructions. Drain, toss in a little olive oil, and set aside.

Melt the butter in a small saucepan set over low heat. Add the flour and cook, stirring, for 1 minute. Gradually pour in the hot milk, whisking constantly, and simmer until the mixture thickens. Stir in the mustard. Let cool slightly. Taste and adjust the seasoning if necessary.

Put the cooked pasta in the prepared baking dish. Pour over the sauce, mushroom mixture, tuna, and parsley and toss to mix well. Spread evenly and sprinkle the seasoned bread crumbs over the top. Bake in the preheated oven for 20–30 minutes, until browned. Serve immediately with a mixed salad.

smoked trout hash with horseradish cream

A perfect dish for two that's speedy to make and satisfying to eat. It could almost be accused of being too simple but the horseradish cream dresses it up nicely. This really is a meal in itself, but you could serve with crusty bread and a peppery watercress salad.

1 lb. baby new potatoes, scrubbed

2 tablespoons unsalted butter

2–3 tablespoons olive oil

1 small red onion, finely chopped

1 celery rib, finely chopped

½ teaspoon paprika

1 tablespoon chopped fresh dill

1 tablespoon grated lemon peel

9 oz. smoked trout, cut in pieces

sea salt and freshly ground black pepper

lemon wedges, to serve

Horseradish cream

4–5 tablespoons sour cream or Greek-style yogurt

2 teaspoons creamed horseradish

a small bunch of fresh chives, snipped

Serves 2

Put the potatoes in a large saucepan with sufficient water to cover. Add a pinch of salt and boil until tender when pierced with a knife. Drain. When cool enough to handle, cut into cubes.

Meanwhile, make the horseradish cream. Combine the sour cream, horseradish, and chives in a small bowl. Mix, cover, and set aside.

Melt the butter and 1 tablespoon of the oil in a large skillet. Add the cubed potatoes with a pinch of salt and cook, stirring occasionally, for about 10 minutes, until browned.

Add the onion, celery, paprika, dill, and lemon peel to the pan and cook, stirring occasionally, for 5 minutes more. Stir in the trout, season, and add a little more oil if the mixture seems dry. Continue cooking, turning every so often, until the hash is well browned.

Serve immediately with the horseradish cream for spooning and lemon wedges.

Variation: Replace the smoked trout with chopped bacon or ham, omit the grated lemon peel, and use parsley in place of the dill. For a vegetarian version, replace the bacon with diced green bell pepper. Serve either variation with a fried egg on top and a dash of Tabasco instead of the horseradish cream.

smoked salmon spaghetti bake with lemon and dill

This is a fantastic dish when you want something elegant but most of all, quick. It is an economical way to serve smoked salmon too as it calls for trimmings, which are just as flavorful as whole slices. This recipe also works with flaked hot smoked salmon if you prefer a richer flavor.

Preheat the oven to 400°F.

Cook the spaghetti according to the package instructions. Drain, toss in a little oil, and set aside.

In a large bowl, combine the half-and-half, sour cream, and egg and whisk to blend. Stir in the salmon, dill, grated lemon peel, ½ teaspoon salt, and peas and mix to blend. Add the cooked spaghetti, toss well to coat, and transfer to the prepared baking dish.

In a small bowl, combine the bread crumbs and Parmesan and season well. Mix then sprinkle over the spaghetti.

Bake in the preheated oven for 25–35 minutes, until just golden. Serve immediately.

14 oz. dried spaghetti

1⅓ cups half-and-half

1 cup sour cream

1 egg, beaten

9 oz. smoked salmon trimmings

a large handful of fresh dill, chopped

1 tablespoon grated lemon peel

½ cup frozen peas

1 generous cup fresh bread crumbs (see note on page 26)

2 tablespoons grated Parmesan

sea salt and freshly ground black pepper

a 12 x 8 inch baking dish, well buttered

Serves 4

baked shrimp and orzo with tomatoes, herbs, and feta

The combination of shrimp and feta has always intrigued me, and this is a recipe I vaguely knew about, but never actually researched until writing this book. It has been adjusted, to be served all in one dish, but try it and you will see it has made the transition very well. Since this is Greek in inspiration, serve with warmed pita bread and a mixed salad made with crisp romaine lettuce, cucumbers, green bell peppers, tomatoes, and black olives. If you prepare the orzo and the tomato sauce ahead, this becomes an unusual and quick weeknight meal, requiring very little effort to assemble and put on the table.

1½ cups orzo (see note on page 50)

2 tablespoons olive oil

1 onion, chopped

2 garlic cloves, crushed

leaves stripped from a few sprigs of fresh oregano, chopped, or 1 teaspoon dried oregano

14-oz. can chopped tomatoes

a pinch of sugar

a pinch of ground allspice

½ cup dry white wine or water

1 cup Greek-style yogurt

7 oz. feta

a small handful of fresh dill, finely chopped

a small handful of fresh basil leaves, shredded

1 lb. large raw shrimp, peeled (fresh or frozen)

a small handful of fresh mint leaves

sea salt and freshly ground black pepper

a 9-inch round baking dish

Serves 4–6

Cook the orzo in a large saucepan of boiling salted water until tender, 12–15 minutes. Drain and set aside.

Put the oil in a large skillet and add the onion. Cook for 3–5 minutes, until soft. Add the garlic, a pinch of salt, and most of the oregano (½ teaspoon if using dried) and cook, stirring for 1 minute. Add the tomatoes, sugar, allspice, and wine. Bring to a boil, then reduce the heat and simmer gently, uncovered, for 10 minutes. Taste and adjust the seasoning if necessary.

Preheat the oven to 400°F.

In a small bowl, stir together the yogurt, half of the feta (crumbled well), and the remaining oregano. Set aside.

Stir in the dill, basil, shrimp, and the remaining feta. Add a good pinch of salt. Transfer to the dish and spread well.

Using a spoon, transfer dollops of the yogurt mixture, and spread on top of the shrimp. This is slightly messy but it is okay to leave a few gaps around the edges and in other places. Sprinkle with the mint leaves and top with a generous grinding of black pepper. Bake in the preheated oven for about 30 minutes, until bubbling around the edges. Serve immediately with a mixed salad.

Moroccan shrimp ragout

It's hard to find a recipe that is quicker to make than this one; it is aromatic, out of the ordinary, and can be on the table in under thirty minutes. Serve with couscous or rice and a crisp green salad.

4 tablespoons olive oil

1–2 shallots, halved and sliced

2 teaspoons ground cumin

1 teaspoon ground ginger

a pinch of ground saffron

1 teaspoon paprika

1 teaspoon harissa paste

2 garlic cloves, finely chopped

14-oz. can chopped tomatoes

1¾ lbs. large raw shrimp, peeled (fresh or frozen)

freshly squeezed juice of ½ a lemon

a large handful of fresh cilantro leaves, chopped

a large handful of fresh flat-leaf parsley leaves, chopped

sea salt and freshly ground black pepper

couscous or rice, to serve

lemon wedges, to serve

Serves 4

Heat the oil in a large skillet. Add the shallots and cook over low heat for 2–3 minutes, until softened. Add the cumin, ginger, saffron, paprika, harissa, and garlic and cook, stirring for 1 minute. Do not let the garlic burn.

Add the tomatoes and ½ cup water and season well. Simmer gently, uncovered, for at least 15 minutes. Taste and adjust the seasoning if necessary. (The recipe can be made in advance up to this point.)

Stir in the shrimp and cook, uncovered, for about 5 minutes, until opaque. Remove from the heat, squeeze over the lemon juice, and add the parsley and cilantro. Mix well and serve immediately spooned over couscous or rice, as preferred, with lemon wedges on the side.

Spanish seafood stew

Here's a one-pot dinner that will fill your kitchen with enticing aromas from faraway places. You will need a deep pot to accommodate all the ingredients, including the mussels at the end. If you do not have one, the mussels can be steamed on their own; simply add them and their cooking liquor into the main dish before serving. The only other requirement is a basket of crusty bread to help mop up the sauce.

1 teaspoon cumin seeds

2 tablespoons olive oil

1 large onion, halved and sliced

2 red bell peppers, halved, seeded, and sliced

4 ripe tomatoes, peeled, seeded, and chopped

2 anchovy fillets, finely chopped

1–2 fresh green chiles, sliced

3 garlic cloves, sliced

3½ lbs. new potatoes, peeled and cut into wedges

1 cup dry white wine

1½ cups fish stock

1 bay leaf

1 lb. live mussels

14 oz. firm-fleshed white fish, such as cod or haddock

8 oz. large raw shrimp, peeled

a large handful of fresh flat-leaf parsley leaves, chopped

sea salt and freshly ground black pepper

rouille (see page 93), to serve

Serves 4

Put the cumin seeds in a small nonstick skillet and dry roast over medium heat until they just turn brown and become aromatic. Crush to a fine powder using a mortar and pestle. Set aside.

Heat the oil in a large, deep pot with a lid. Add the onion and bell peppers and cook for 3–5 minutes, until soft. Add the tomatoes, anchovies, chiles, garlic, toasted cumin seeds, and potatoes. Season with salt and stir to combine.

Add the wine, stock, and bay leaf. Bring to a boil and cook for 1 minute, then lower the heat and simmer gently, uncovered, for 20–30 minutes, until the potatoes are tender when pierced with a knife. Taste for seasoning and adjust if necessary. (Up to this point, the recipe can be made one day in advance.)

Clean and debeard the mussels and discard any that do not close. Stir in the fish and shrimp and cook until just opaque. Increase the heat to high. Add the mussels on top, cover and cook for 2–3 minutes, until the mussels open. (Discard any that do not open.)

Sprinkle with the parsley and serve, with the rouille for spooning on top and plenty of crusty bread.

seafood lasagne

A decadent version of a family favorite, this lasagne has shellfish, spinach, and a béchamel made even richer with mascarpone. It makes a pleasant change from the classic meat recipe and is perfect for summer eating. Serve with a salad dressed with tangy vinaigrette.

2 tablespoons olive oil

1 onion, chopped

1 celery rib, diced

2 garlic cloves, finely chopped

½ teaspoon dried hot pepper flakes

a sprig of fresh thyme

a large handful of fresh flat-leaf parsley leaves, chopped

14 oz. mixed seafood (shrimp, scallops, and squid rings)

½ cup dry white wine

2¾ cups passata (Italian strained tomatoes) or tomato purée

a pinch of sugar

8 sheets green lasagne

3 tablespoons freshly grated Parmesan

sea salt and freshly ground black pepper

For the béchamel

3 tablespoons unsalted butter

¼ cup all-purpose flour

2½ cups hot milk

2 tablespoons grated Parmesan

3 tablespoons mascarpone

a pinch of ground nutmeg

7 oz. frozen leaf spinach, defrosted

a 12 x 8 inch baking dish

Serves 4–6

Preheat the oven to 375°F.

Heat the oil in a large skillet. Add the onion and celery and cook over low heat for 3–5 minutes, until soft. Stir in the garlic, pepper flakes, thyme, and parsley and season generously with salt. Cook, stirring, for 1 minute. Add the seafood and cook, stirring, for 1 minute. Add the wine and cook for 1 minute more. Add the passata, season with salt, and add the sugar. Stir to blend and simmer gently, uncovered, for 15 minutes.

To make the béchamel, melt the butter in a heavy-based saucepan set over low heat. Stir in the flour and cook, stirring constantly, for 1 minute. Add the hot milk gradually, whisking constantly, and continue whisking gently for 3–5 minutes, until the sauce begins to thicken. Season and stir in the Parmesan and mascarpone until blended. Stir in the nutmeg and spinach.

To assemble, spoon a thin layer of the seafood sauce on the bottom of the baking dish. Return any bits of seafood to the sauce; you just want a thin layer of tomato base for the pasta to sit on. Top with 2 sheets of lasagne. Spread half of the seafood sauce on top, spreading evenly right up to the edges and distribute the seafood evenly on top. Top with 2 sheets of lasagne. Spread half of the béchamel sauce on top, spreading evenly right up to the edges. Continue layering (lasagne, seafood, lasagne, béchamel) and finish with the béchamel.

Sprinkle with the Parmesan and bake in the preheated oven for 25–25 minutes, until just browned. Serve immediately.

vegetarian

baked rigatoni with mozzarella

Blissfully simple to make, with virtuous quantities of vegetables, this is a good way to eat well with minimal effort. And putting the mozzarella in the middle as well as on top means you get a lovely inner layer of melting cheese, as well as a browned topping. Other vegetables can be used according to what's in season or to hand—corn, broccoli, spinach, and zucchini will all work nicely. The important thing is to chop all the vegetables into dice of the same size, to allow them to nestle inside the pasta shapes.

3 tablespoons olive oil

1 small onion, diced

1 carrot, finely diced

2–3 celery ribs, from the inner section, with leaves, diced

1 small red, yellow or orange bell pepper, seeded and diced

4 oz. mushrooms, diced

3 garlic cloves, finely chopped

½ cup dry white or red wine

½–1 teaspoon dried hot pepper flakes, to taste

½ tablespoon fresh thyme leaves or 1 teaspoon dried thyme

a large handful of fresh parsley or basil leaves, finely chopped

14-oz. can chopped tomatoes

2¾ cups passata (Italian strained tomatoes) or tomato purée

a pinch of sugar

1 lb. dried rigatoni

1 lb. mozzarella, sliced

sea salt and freshly ground black pepper

a 12 x 8 inch baking dish, well oiled

Serves 4–6

Heat the oil in a large saucepan, add the onion, and cook over low heat for 3–5 minutes, until soft. Add the carrot, celery, and bell pepper. Season and cook for 2–3 minutes. Stir in the mushrooms and garlic and cook for 1 minute more. Add the wine and cook for 1 minute more. Stir in the pepper flakes, thyme, parsley, tomatoes, passata, and sugar. Season generously and stir to mix. Reduce the heat and simmer, uncovered, for 20–30 minutes. Taste and adjust the seasoning if necessary.

Meanwhile, cook the pasta according to the package instructions until al dente. Drain well and set aside.

Preheat the oven to 400°F.

Combine the cooked pasta and the vegetable sauce and mix well. Spread half the pasta in the prepared dish evenly. Top with half of the mozzarella. Top with the remaining pasta in an even layer and arrange the remaining mozzarella slices on top.

Bake in the preheated oven for 25–30 minutes, until the cheese melts and bubbles. Serve immediately.

vegetable enchiladas

Homemade enchiladas are so much easier to make than you think and very delicious.

2 tablespoons olive oil

1 lb. zucchini, diced

1 red onion, diced

1 cup sweetcorn kernels, canned or frozen

½ fresh red or green chile, halved, seeded, and sliced

1 teaspoon ground cumin

14-oz. can black beans, drained

a large handful of fresh cilantro leaves, chopped

8 corn tortillas

2 cups grated mild cheddar

sour cream, to serve

For the sauce

1 onion, coarsely chopped

2 garlic cloves

2 tablespoons olive oil

1–2 teaspoons dried hot pepper flakes, to taste

½ teaspoon Spanish hot smoked paprika (pimentón picante) or cayenne pepper

1 teaspoon ground cumin

1 teaspoon dried oregano

2¾ cups passata (Italian strained tomatoes) or tomato purée

1 vegetable bouillon cube diluted in 1½ cups hot water

sea salt and freshly ground black pepper

a 14 x 10 inch baking dish

Serves 4

Preheat the oven to 400°F.

To make the sauce, put the onion and garlic in a food processor and pulse until finely chopped. Transfer to a skillet. Add the oil and cook over low heat, stirring, for 3–5 minutes, until just soft. Stir in the pepper flakes, paprika, cumin, and oregano and add salt to taste. Cook, stirring, for 2 minutes. Add the passata and bouillon and simmer gently, uncovered, for at least 15 minutes. Let cool slightly.

Meanwhile, make the filling. Heat the oil in a large saucepan, add the zucchini and onion and cook over low heat for 5–8 minutes, until just tender. Stir in the corn, chile, cumin, and beans and season to taste. Remove from the heat and stir in the cilantro, reserving some to garnish.

To assemble, warm the tortillas according to the package instructions. Coat the bottom of a baking dish with a layer of the tomato sauce. Working one at a time, dab a tortilla gently in the warm sauce in the pan, just to coat the bottom side, then turn over to coat the other side. (If you use tongs for this, be careful not to tear the tortillas.)

Transfer the coated tortilla to a plate and fill with a large spoonful of filling, a handful of grated cheese, then fold the tortilla over to enclose the filling and transfer it in a baking dish, seam-side down. Continue until all the tortillas have been filled. Spoon the remaining sauce over the tortillas, concentrating on the ends as these tend to dry out. Sprinkle the remaining cheese down the center.

Bake in the preheated oven for 15–20 minutes, until the cheese has melted. Sprinkle with the reserved cilantro and serve with sour cream on the side.

zucchini gratin with fresh herbs and goat cheese

A classic of French home cooking, this gratin includes a topping of tangy goat cheese. If you grow your own herbs, add whatever is available: savory, majoram, oregano, or any other soft-leaved herb, the more the merrier. This is perfect, simply served with a mixed salad of lettuce and ripe tomatoes and a big basket of fresh crusty bread.

1 cup heavy cream

leaves from a small bunch of fresh flat-leaf parsley, finely chopped

a small bunch of chives, snipped

a pinch of freshly grated nutmeg

¾ cup grated Gruyère

3¼ lbs. zucchini, very thinly sliced

5½ oz. soft goat cheese

sea salt and freshly ground black pepper

a 10-inch round, deep-sided baking dish, well buttered

Serves 4

Preheat the oven to 375°F.

Put the cream, parsley, chives, nutmeg, salt, and pepper in a small bowl and whisk together. Add half the Gruyère.

Arrange half the zucchini slices in the prepared baking dish, sprinkle with the remaining Gruyère and season with a little salt. Top with the remaining zucchini slices, season again, and pour over the cream mixture. Crumble the goat cheese over the top.

Bake in the preheated oven for 35–45 minutes, until browned. Serve immediately with a mixed salad and plenty of crusty bread.

Note: If preferred, you can make the gratin in 4 individual dishes, simply reduce the cooking time by about 5–10 minutes.

root vegetable gratin

There is something very satisfying and tranquil about preparing this recipe. So if the thought of peeling and slicing these vegetables puts you off, think again. It sounds perhaps more daunting than it really is; but you will be done in no time, and it will be well worth the effort. This is a very simple dish, very impressive and hugely delightful. Serve with a cheese platter, crusty bread, and a green salad.

Preheat the oven to 400°F.

Put all the vegetable slices in a large bowl and toss gently to combine. Set aside.

Combine the cream, crème fraîche, and milk in a small saucepan and heat just to melt the crème fraîche. Stir well, season with salt and pepper.

Arrange half of the vegetables slices in the prepared baking dish. Sprinkle with a little salt and one-third of the cheese. Pour over one-third of the cream mixture. Top with the rest of the vegetable slices, the remaining cheese, and a sprinkle of salt. Pour over the remaining cream mixture and bake in the preheated oven for 1–1½ hours, until browned on top. Serve immediately.

3 small turnips (about 13 oz.), peeled, halved, and very thinly sliced

½ a celeriac (about 11 oz.), peeled, halved, and very thinly sliced

½ a swede (about 1 lb.), peeled, halved, and very thinly sliced

1½ lbs. waxy potatoes, peeled, halved and very thinly sliced

1 scant cup heavy cream

6 tablespoons crème fraîche or sour cream

1 cup milk

1½ cups grated Gruyère or medium cheddar, grated

sea salt and freshly ground black pepper

a 12 x 8 inch baking dish, very well buttered

Serves 4–6

ravioli bake with grilled sweet peppers

An easy dish made with my favorite freezer staple: mixed grilled bell peppers. These are fantastic for stirring into anything that needs a lift but if you cannot find any, simply thinly slice a red and a yellow bell pepper and sweat it with the onions. This is meant to be simple, so I've kept the ingredient list short, but some sliced mushrooms and/or pitted black olives make a pleasant addition if you have some to hand. Fresh or dried ravioli both work well here, and any filling will do, but goat cheese and pesto is an especially good one. Serve with a simple green salad.

2 tablespoons olive oil

1 onion, halved and sliced

8 oz. frozen mixed grilled bell peppers, or 1 red and 1 yellow bell pepper, seeded and sliced (see recipe introduction)

3 garlic cloves, crushed

1 teaspoon dried thyme

¼–½ teaspoon dried hot pepper flakes, to taste

2 x 14-oz. cans chopped tomatoes

a pinch of sugar

a large handful of fresh basil or flat-leaf parsley leaves, chopped

1 lb. small filled ravioli or cappeletti

⅔ cup grated Gruyère or medium cheddar

2 tablespoons grated Parmesan

sea salt and freshly ground black pepper

a 13 x 8 inch baking dish, lightly oiled

Serves 4–6

Preheat the oven to 400°F.

Heat the oil in a large saucepan. Add the onion and cook over low heat for 3–5 minutes, until soft. Add the peppers, garlic, thyme, and pepper flakes and cook, stirring, for 2–3 minutes. Stir in the tomatoes and sugar, season and simmer, uncovered, for 15 minutes. Taste and adjust the seasoning if necessary. Stir in the basil.

Cook the ravioli according to the package instructions and drain well.

Tip the cooked ravioli into the sauce and stir gently to coat. Transfer to the prepared baking dish, spread evenly, and sprinkle both the cheeses over the top.

Bake in the preheated oven for 20–30 minutes, until the cheese is melted and golden. Serve immediately with a green salad.

artichoke, mushroom, and olive pasta bake with provolone

Here is a great vegetarian dish, with so much flavor no one will miss the meat! This recipe calls for provolone which is a smoked Italian cheese, but almost any cheese can be used so experiment with different types—Gruyère is a great one here, as is smoked mozzarella, soft goat cheese, or even sharp cheddar. Serve with a crisp green salad.

2–3 tablespoons olive oil

1 onion, finely chopped

½ teaspoon dried oregano

½ teaspoon dried thyme

5 oz. white mushrooms, coarsely chopped

4 garlic cloves, crushed

¼ teaspoon dried hot pepper flakes

½ cup dry white or red wine

2 x 14-oz. cans chopped tomatoes

14-oz can artichoke hearts, drained and sliced

½ cup pitted black olives, sliced

a pinch of sugar

14 oz. dried tube pasta, such as penne or rigatoni

6 oz. provolone, cubed

Béchamel sauce

3 tablespoons unsalted butter

¼ cup all-purpose flour

2½ cups hot milk

4 tablespoons grated Parmesan

sea salt and freshly ground black pepper

a 12 x 8 inch baking dish

Serves 4

Heat 1 tablespoon of the oil in a large skillet. Add the onion and cook over low heat for about 5 minutes, until soft. Stir in the oregano, thyme, and mushrooms and cook for 2–3 minutes more, adding a little more oil if required. Stir in the garlic and pepper flakes and season with salt. Cook for 1 minute, then add the wine. Cook for 1 minute more, then add the tomatoes, artichokes, and olives. Add the sugar, season, stir to combine, and simmer for about 15 minutes. Taste and adjust the seasoning if necessary.

Preheat the oven to 400°F.

To prepare the béchamel sauce, melt the butter in a heavy-based saucepan set over low heat. Add the flour and cook, stirring, for 1 minute. Slowly pour in the hot milk, whisking continuously, and simmer until the mixture thickens. Season well. Stir in 2 tablespoons of the Parmesan and set aside.

Cook the pasta according the package instructions until just al dente. Drain and set aside.

To assemble, spread a small amount of the tomato mixture over the bottom of the baking dish and add 1 tablespoon of the oil. Arrange about one-third of the cooked pasta in a single layer on the bottom. Top with half of the remaining tomato mixture and spread evenly. Cover with another layer of pasta (using half of the remaining amount.) Spoon over half of the béchamel and spread evenly. Top with the provolone, spacing the pieces evenly. Spoon the remaining tomato mixture on top. Top with the remaining pasta and béchamel. Sprinkle with the remaining Parmesan. Bake in the preheated oven for about 30–40 minutes, until browned. Serve immediately.

butternut squash, corn, and bread pudding with cheese and chives

Inspiration for this recipe comes from an old, well-worn vegetarian cookbook of mine. It is a recipe for an English-style savory bread pudding, but adding a few vegetables makes it more of a meal, and the sweetness of the squash and corn go well with the creamy, cheesy bread part. In place of the baguette, you could save up the ends from sliced loaves. And, any kind of cheese can be used here, as can a combination of cheeses, so it's a good way to use up odds and ends. Serve with a mixed salad.

1 tablespoon olive oil

1 large onion, halved and thinly sliced

1½ cups milk

1 cup light cream

3 eggs, beaten

a small bunch of chives, snipped

leaves from a small bunch of fresh parsley, finely chopped

1 baguette, cut into ¼-inch slices

2 cups corn kernels, canned or frozen

about 1 lb. peeled and sliced butternut squash

1 cup grated sharp cheddar

sea salt and freshly ground black pepper

a 12 x 8 inch baking dish, very well buttered

Serves 4–6

Preheat the oven to 375°F.

Heat the oil in a large skillet. Add the onion and cook over low heat for 3–5 minutes, until soft. Season lightly and set aside.

Combine the milk, cream, and eggs in a small bowl and whisk to combine. Season with 1½ teaspoons salt. Add the chives and parsley, mix well and set aside.

Arrange half the baguette slices in the prepared baking dish in a single layer; you may need to tear some to cover all the space. Put half of the onion slices on top, then scatter over half of the corn. Arrange half of the squash slices evenly on top and sprinkle with half of the cheese. Repeat one more time (bread, onion, corn, squash, cheese.) Stir the milk mixture and pour it evenly all over the pudding.

Cover tightly with foil and bake in the preheated oven for 20 minutes. Remove the foil and continue baking for about 30–40 minutes, until golden. Serve immediately.

Provençal eggplant, tomato, and onion bake

This indulgent French vegetable dish improves with time so perfect for making ahead, or cooking extra for leftovers. A bowl of pasta tossed with cream and finely grated Parmesan is the perfect accompaniment.

about ½ cup olive oil

4 garlic cloves, crushed

14-oz. can chopped tomatoes

a pinch of sugar

1 tablespoon chopped fresh parsley leaves

a pinch of cayenne pepper

4 medium eggplants, sliced

¾ cup fresh bread crumbs (see note on page 26)

leaves stripped from 2 sprigs of fresh thyme or 1 teaspoon dried thyme

2 large onions, thickly sliced

3 large or 5 medium fresh plum tomatoes, sliced

leaves from 2 sprigs of fresh basil, finely chopped

sea salt and freshly ground black pepper

a 12 x 8 inch baking dish

Serves 4–6

Heat 1 tablespoon of the oil in a saucepan. Add the garlic and cook over medium heat for 1 minute; taking care not to let it burn. Add the tomatoes, sugar, parsley, and cayenne and season well. Simmer, uncovered, for at least 15 minutes.

Preheat the oven to 400°F.

Bring a large saucepan of salted water to a boil and add the eggplant. Cook for 3–5 minutes, to blanch. Remove and pat dry on paper towels.

Combine the bread crumbs and thyme leaves in a small bowl and season. Toss to mix and set aside.

Drizzle 2–3 tablespoons of oil in the baking dish and spread evenly. Arrange the eggplant slices on top and drizzle with some more oil. Arrange the onion slices on top and season. Spoon the tomato mixture on top of the onions and spread evenly. Arrange the tomato slices on top and sprinkle with the bread crumb mixture.

Bake in the preheated oven for about 45 minutes, until browned. Serve hot or warm.

couscous with seven vegetables

This is a vegetarian version of a traditional Moroccan dish, which is meant to be highly aromatic and slightly sweet. It can be made with other vegetables: pumpkin, squash, and turnips are all suitable additions, but seven vegetables is considered good luck so if you experiment with others be sure to maintain the numbers. It is a meal in itself but you could also serve it to accompany simply grilled chicken.

3 zucchini, halved and quartered lengthwise

3 large fresh plum tomatoes, halved and seeded

1 red bell pepper, cored, seeded, and quartered

1 yellow bell pepper, cored, seeded, and quartered

1–2 tablespoons olive oil

4 cups vegetable stock

a pinch of saffron threads

½ teaspoon turmeric

1 teaspoon ground white pepper

½ teaspoon cinnamon

1 teaspoon ground ginger

a small bunch of fresh cilantro, tied firmly in a bundle with string

3 large onions, quartered

4 large carrots, peeled, halved, and quartered

1 lb. rutabaga, peeled and cubed

7-oz. can chickpeas, drained

a large handful of raisins

1–2 teaspoons harissa paste, to taste

freshly squeezed lemon juice

1½ cups couscous

sea salt

Serves 4

Preheat the oven to 425°F.

Arrange the zucchini, tomatoes, and bell peppers in a large roasting pan. Drizzle with the oil and toss to coat. Spread out in a single layer, sprinkle lightly with salt, and roast in the preheated oven for 20–30 minutes, until browned. Remove from the oven, transfer the vegetables to a plate, cover with foil to keep warm and set aside.

Meanwhile combine the stock, saffron, turmeric, pepper, cinnamon, ginger, cilantro bundle, onions, carrots, and rutabaga in a large saucepan. Top up with a bit more water if necessary; the vegetables should be covered but not completely submerged. Season with salt and bring to a boil, then reduce the heat and simmer gently, uncovered, for about 30 minutes. Stir in the chickpeas and raisins and continue simmering for 10–15 minutes, until the vegetables are tender and the liquid has reduced by about one-third.

Meanwhile prepare the couscous according to the package instructions. Cover with foil and keep warm in a low oven until ready to serve.

Use a slotted spoon to transfer the stewed vegetables to the plate with the roasted vegetables and toss gently to combine. Add the harissa paste and a squeeze of lemon juice to the broth in the saucepan and stir to blend. Taste and adjust the seasoning if necessary. Pour the broth over the vegetables and serve them spooned over the couscous.

roasted butternut squash with spiced lentils, goat cheese, and walnuts

This recipe will fill your kitchen with appetizing and exotic aromas. You can use pumpkin or sweet potato in place of the squash, or a combination of the two, as long as the weight is roughly the same as that of a butternut squash. Sometimes I add a handful of canned chickpeas during the last bit of simmering. Serve with plenty of crusty bread.

1⅓ cups green lentils, rinsed and drained

¼ cup walnut pieces

1 butternut squash, peeled, seeded, and cubed

3 tablespoons olive oil

1 large onion, halved and sliced

1 fresh red chile, halved, seeded, and sliced

1 teaspoon ground cumin

1 teaspoon ground turmeric

1 teaspoon paprika

2 garlic cloves, crushed

14-oz. can chopped tomatoes

a pinch of sugar

a large handful of fresh flat-leaf parsley leaves, chopped

a small handful of fresh cilantro leaves, finely chopped

freshly squeezed juice of ½ a lemon

8 oz. soft goat cheese or feta

sea salt and freshly ground black pepper

Serves 4

Preheat the oven to 375°F.

Put the lentils in a saucepan with sufficient cold water to cover. Add a pinch of salt, bring to a boil, and simmer for 20–30 minutes, until tender. Drain and set aside.

Dry roast the walnuts in a small nonstick skillet set over low heat, until browned. Set aside.

Arrange the squash cubes on a baking sheet, toss with 2 tablespoons of the oil, and sprinkle with a little salt. Roast in the preheated oven for 30–35 minutes, until tender, turning halfway through cooking time.

Heat the remaining oil in a large saucepan, add the onion and cook over low heat for 3–5 minutes, until soft. Add the chile, cumin, turmeric, paprika, garlic, and a pinch of salt and cook, stirring for 1 minute. Add the tomatoes, sugar, another pinch of salt, half the parsley, and half the cilantro. Simmer, uncovered, for 20 minutes, stirring in the cooked lentils about 5 minutes before the end of cooking time, just to warm through. Taste and adjust the seasoning if necessary.

Add the roasted squash, the remaining herbs, and a squeeze of lemon juice. Taste and adjust the seasoning. Crumble over the goat cheese, add the walnuts, and serve immediately with plenty of crusty bread.

wild mushroom and potato ragout with leeks

So many potato recipes are baked or roasted, but it's nice to have a stovetop preparation. This one is a lovely, fall dish that is quick to throw together, so perfect for a midweek supper, just the thing when days and nights are getting cooler. Chanterelles are a favorite mushroom, but any kind can be used here, including dried wild mushrooms, but these will need to be soaked in warm water beforehand.

2¼ lbs. new potatoes

2 tablespoons olive oil

1 onion, halved and sliced

1 trimmed leek, thinly sliced into rounds

2 tablespoons unsalted butter

10 oz. chanterelle mushrooms, cut into bite-size pieces

2 garlic cloves, crushed

1 teaspoon dried thyme

1⅔ cups vegetable stock

1 bay leaf

2 tablespoons crème fraîche or sour cream

a large handful of fresh flat-leaf parsley leaves, chopped

sea salt and freshly ground black pepper

Serves 4

Put the potatoes in a large saucepan with sufficient water to cover. Add a pinch of salt and bring to a boil. Cook until tender when pierced with a knife. When cool enough to handle, cut into large dice.

Heat the oil in a large saucepan and add the onion and leek. Season lightly and cook over medium heat for 2–3 minutes, until soft.

Add the butter and stir until melted. Add the mushrooms, garlic, and thyme. Cook, stirring, for 1–2 minutes. Season lightly, then add the stock, bay leaf, and cooked potatoes. Add a little water to just cover if necessary.

Simmer, uncovered, for 30–40 minutes, until the liquid has reduced by half. Taste and adjust the seasoning if necessary. Stir in the crème fraîche and parsley and serve immediately.

cannellini bean and cabbage gratin

This is good, reliable comfort food, ideal for adding a bit of warmth on a chilly evening. This makes a good vegetarian entrée but is also a nice companion for sausages, roast pork, or even duck. Although there are carrots in the recipe, I find this works well with a few more on the side, either roasted or mashed with a little butter.

Bring a large saucepan water to a boil. Add the cabbage and a pinch of salt and cook for 5–8 minutes, until just blanched. Drain and set aside.

Heat the oil in a large skillet. Add the onion and cook over low heat for 3–5 minutes, until soft. Add the carrots and celery and cook for 5 minutes more. Season well, add the garlic, and cook for 1 minute. Add the beans, thyme, bay leaf, rosemary, sage, and wine. Bring to a boil and simmer, uncovered, for about 10 minutes, until the liquid has almost reduced.

In a small bowl, mix the bread crumbs and Parmesan and season well. Set aside.

Preheat the oven to 400°F.

Core and chop the blanched cabbage and add to the beans with the stock. Cover and simmer for 10 minutes, then uncover and simmer until the liquid is reduced by half. Stir in the crème fraîche. Taste and adjust the seasoning if necessary.

Transfer the mixture to the baking dish and spread evenly. Arrange the tomato slices on top and sprinkle over the seasoned bread crumbs. Bake in the preheated oven for about 20–25 minutes, until browned. Serve immediately.

½ a savoy cabbage, cut in half

2 tablespoons olive oil

1 onion, chopped

2 carrots, peeled and sliced

2 celery ribs, sliced

4 garlic cloves, sliced

2 x 14-oz. cans cannellini beans, drained

½ teaspoon dried thyme

1 bay leaf

leaves from a sprig of fresh rosemary or sage (or both)

½ cup dry white wine

1 cup fresh bread crumbs (see note on page 26)

2 tablespoons grated Parmesan

1¼ cups vegetable stock

2 tablespoons crème fraîche or sour cream

5 fresh plum tomatoes, sliced

sea salt and freshly ground black pepper

a 10-inch round baking dish

Serves 4–6

Greek summer vegetable stew with lemon and olives

Any kind of olive can be used here but if you can find some marinated with whole coriander seeds, these are the best ones to use. This is a summer stew and is best eaten lukewarm or at room temperature. Serve with a salad made from romaine lettuce dressed with extra virgin olive oil and lemon juice, some feta, and crusty bread.

2 tablespoons olive oil

1 onion, chopped

1 lb. small new potatoes (red if available), cubed

12 oz. zucchini, halved and quartered lengthwise, then sliced thickly

3 garlic cloves, sliced

¼ teaspoon paprika

¼ teaspoon cayenne pepper

2 x 14-oz. cans chopped tomatoes

leaves from a small bunch of parsley, finely chopped

sprigs from a small bunch of dill, finely chopped

9 oz. fine green beans (haricots verts), halved

¾ cup cracked green olives, pitted

freshly squeezed juice of ½ a lemon

sea salt and freshly ground black pepper

Serves 4–6

Heat the oil in a large saucepan. Add the onion and cook over low heat for 3–5 minutes, until soft. Add the potatoes, zucchini, garlic, paprika, cayenne, and a pinch of salt and cook, stirring to coat in the oil, for 1 minute.

Add the tomatoes, parsley, and half the dill. Stir to combine and add some water to thin slightly; about ½ cup should be enough. Season well, then cover and simmer for 30 minutes.

Add the green beans, cover, and continue to simmer for about 20 minutes more, until the beans are tender. Stir in the olives, lemon juice, and remaining dill. Taste and adjust the seasoning if necessary. Serve at room temperature with a simple salad of romaine lettuce, some feta, and plenty of crusty bread.

sweet potato, spinach, and chickpea stew with coconut

This falls somewhere between a stew and a soup, but I like to make use of the abundant sauce and serve with fragrant jasmine rice. If you like things spicy, add two chiles and all their seeds; if not, add one and keep the seeds out. It will be very mild and the specks of red are pretty against the orange.

1 tablespoon vegetable oil

1 onion, halved and sliced

2-inch piece of fresh ginger, peeled and grated

1–2 fresh red chiles, halved and sliced

1 teaspoon curry powder

1 teaspoon ground cumin

3 lbs. sweet potatoes, peeled and cubed

14-oz. can coconut milk

1¾ cups vegetable stock

1 tablespoon Thai fish sauce (optional)

14-oz. can chickpeas, drained

8 oz. fresh baby spinach leaves, washed

sea salt

jasmine rice, to serve

Serves 4–6

Heat the oil in a large saucepan. Add the onion and cook over low heat for 3–5 minutes, until just soft. Add the ginger, chiles, curry powder, cumin, and a pinch of salt. Cook for 1–2 minutes, stirring, until aromatic.

Add the sweet potatoes and stir to coat in the spices. Add the coconut milk and stock and a little water if necessary, just to cover the sweet potatoes; the mixture should be soupy as it will cook down. Add the fish sauce (if using) or some salt, if preferred. Bring to a boil, then simmer, uncovered, for 15 minutes.

Add the chickpeas and continue to simmer for 15–20 minutes more, until the sweet potatoes are tender.

Add the spinach, in batches, stirring to blend and waiting for each batch to wilt before adding the next. Taste and adjust the seasoning if necessary. Serve immediately with jasmine rice.

winter vegetable bake

This is really three recipes in one dish: a potato gratin, cauliflower cheese, and roasted Brussels sprouts. The result is a substantial and filling dish that's good served with crusty bread and a salad of robust winter greens. That said, nothing should stop you from serving this alongside a Sunday roast.

Preheat the oven to 400°F.

Toss the Brussels sprouts with the oil until coated, season with salt, and spread out in a single layer on a baking sheet. Roast in the preheated oven for 25–30 minutes, until just tender.

Meanwhile, bring a large saucepan of water to a boil. Add the cauliflower florets and a pinch of salt and blanch for 5–8 minutes, until just tender. Drain. When cool enough to handle, slice thinly and set aside.

Bring another large saucepan of salted water to a boil, add the potatoes, and cook until just tender when pierced with a knife but not cooked through. Drain. When cool enough to handle, slice the potatoes thinly and set aside.

In a bowl, whisk together the crème fraîche and light cream and season well. The mixture should be thick, but still liquid enough to pour—add a spoonful or so of milk to thin if required. Set aside. Season the bread crumbs and stir in the paprika. Set aside.

Arrange the potato slices in the prepared baking dish and lay the onion slices on top. Sprinkle with salt and half of the cheese. Arrange the cauliflower slices on top of the cheese, then sprinkle with the remaining cheese. Pour over the cream mixture. Top with the roasted Brussels sprouts in an even layer, including any leaves that break off. Cover with foil and bake in the preheated oven for 30 minutes. After 30 minutes, remove from the oven. Remove the foil, sprinkle with the bread crumbs and Parmesan and continue baking, uncovered, for a further 30–40 minutes, until well browned. Serve immediately.

10 oz. Brussels sprouts, trimmed and quartered

2–3 tablespoons olive oil

1 lb. cauliflower florets (about 1 medium head)

1½ lbs. waxy potatoes

¾ cup crème fraîche or sour cream

½ cup light cream

½ cup fresh bread crumbs (see note on page 26)

a pinch of paprika

1 onion, halved and thinly sliced

1½ cups grated sharp cheddar

3 tablespoons grated Parmesan

sea salt and freshly ground black pepper

a 12 x 8 inch baking dish, very well buttered

Serves 4–6

ratatouille

Although this is unashamedly olive oil laden, it shouldn't be greasy, which is difficult as eggplants tend to soak up as much oil as they are given like a sponge. This is why I microwave the eggplants to pre-cook them and keep oil absorption to a minimum. Light steaming will have the same effect if you don't have a microwave. Serve with rice and a little grated cheese to make a meal. I always seem to have an awkwardly small amount of ratatouille left, which is happily just enough to fill an omelet or savory crêpe for two.

2¼ lbs. eggplants, cut into cubes

6–7 tablespoons olive oil

2 onions, coarsely chopped

2 red bell peppers, halved, seeded, and cut into pieces

2 yellow bell peppers, halved, seeded, and cut into pieces

1 green bell pepper, halved, seeded, and cut into pieces

1½ lbs. zucchini halved lengthwise and sliced

6 fresh plum tomatoes, halved, seeded, and chopped

6 garlic cloves, crushed

a large handful of fresh basil leaves, coarsely chopped

sea salt and freshly ground black pepper

rice, to serve (optional)

Serves 4–6

Put the eggplant cubes in a microwave-proof bowl with 3 tablespoons cold water and microwave on high for 6 minutes. Drain and set aside.

Heat 3 tablespoons of the oil in a large saucepan. Add the onions and cook over low heat for 3–5 minutes, until soft. Season with a little salt.

Add the bell peppers and cook for a further 5–8 minutes, stirring occasionally. Season with a little salt.

Add 1 more tablespoon of the oil and then the zucchini. Mix well and cook for 5 minutes more. Season with a little more salt.

Add 2 more tablespoons of the oil and the drained eggplants. Cook, stirring often, for 5 minutes more. Add the tomatoes, 5 of the garlic cloves, half of the basil, and 1 more tablespoon of the oil, if required. Check the seasoning and adjust if necessary. Cook for 5 minutes. Cover, reduce the heat, and simmer gently for 30 minutes, stirring occasionally.

Stir in the remaining garlic and basil just before serving. Serve with rice or crusty bread, as preferred.

index

conversion chart

Volume equivalents:

American	Metric	Imperial
6 tbsp butter	85 g	3 oz.
7 tbsp butter	100 g	3½ oz.
1 stick butter	115 g	4 oz.
1 teaspoon	5 ml	
1 tablespoon	15 ml	
¼ cup	60 ml	2 fl.oz.
⅓ cup	75 ml	2½ fl.oz.
½ cup	125 ml	4 fl.oz.
⅔ cup	150 ml	5 fl.oz. (¼ pint)
¾ cup	175 ml	6 fl.oz.
1 cup	250 ml	8 fl.oz.

Oven temperatures:

120°C/130°C	(250°F)	Gas ½
140°C	(275°F)	Gas 1
150°C	(300°F)	Gas 2
160°C/170°C	(325°F)	Gas 3
180°C	(350°F)	Gas 4
190°C	(375°F)	Gas 5
200°C	(400°F)	Gas 6
220°C	(425°F)	Gas 7

Weight equivalents:		**Measurements:**	
Imperial	Metric	Inches	Cm
1 oz.	30 g	¼ inch	0.5 cm
2 oz.	55 g	½ inch	1 cm
3 oz.	85 g	¾ inch	1.5 cm
3½ oz.	100 g	1 inch	2.5 cm
4 oz.	115 g	2 inches	5 cm
5 oz.	140 g	3 inches	7 cm
6 oz.	175 g	4 inches	10 cm
8 oz. (½ lb.)	225 g	5 inches	12 cm
9 oz.	250 g	6 inches	15 cm
10 oz.	280 g	7 inches	18 cm
11½ oz.	325 g	8 inches	20 cm
12 oz.	350 g	9 inches	23 cm
13 oz.	375 g	10 inches	25 cm
14 oz.	400 g	11 inches	28 cm
15 oz.	425 g	12 inches	30 cm
16 oz. (1 lb.)	450 g		